the cocktail
handbook

the cocktail

handbook

Maria Costantino

ISLAND BOOKS

First published in 2001 by D&S Books Limited

© 2001 D&S Books Limited

D&S Books Limited
Cottage Meadow, Bocombe,
Parkham, Bideford
Devon, England
EX39 5PH

e-mail us at:-
enquiries@dsbooks.fsnet.co.uk

This edition reprinted in 2002 by
S.WEBB & SON (Distributors) LTD
Telford Place, Pentraeth Road, Menai Bridge,
Isle of Anglesey, LL59 5RW

ISBN 1-903327-32-6

Creative Director: Sarah King
Editor: Judith Millidge
Project Editor: Clare Howarth-Maden
Photographer: Colin Bowling
Designer: Axis Design

Printed in China

3 5 7 9 10 8 6 4 2

contents

Introduction

The word 'cocktail' inevitably conjures up images of the 'speakeasies' of the Prohibition era, of sharp-suited gangsters and elegantly dressed molls, and of the Bright Young Things of the Jazz Age. While the golden age of the cocktail was undoubtedly the 1920s and 1930s, the practice of serving 'mixed drinks' is much older.

Alcoholic mixed drinks called braggets made of ale and mead (fermented honey) are known to have been popular in the 14th century, while mint julep is believed to have been made first in 18th century Virginia and served as a morning eye-opener.

Over the last 200 years many stories have emerged to explain the origin of the term cocktail. In his 1933 work, *The Cocktail Book – A Sideboard Manual for Gentlemen*, John MacQueen tells the legend of the cock's tail and of the lovely young girl called Daisy who invented it. The story goes that during the American War of Independence, the innkeeper of the Bunch of Grapes and a keen fan of the bloody sport of cock-fighting, discovered that Jupiter, his prize bird, was missing. Some time later, a young officer rode into town with Jupiter under his arm. Squire Allen was delighted to have his bird returned and ordered Daisy to serve the soldier the finest refreshment. A toast was drunk to 'the cock's tail', since the mighty Jupiter had not lost a single feather during his absence.

Myths and legends

Other stories say that the cocktail was derived from the French word *coquetier* (egg cup). Monsieur Antoine Peychaud, a chemist in New Orleans, is said to have served his guests mixed drinks in egg cups. A mixed drink called a 'coquetel' was taken to America by the Marquis de Lafayette in 1777 and French officers in George Washington's army were said to enjoy the 'concoction' of wines. In 1779, Betsy Flanagan, the widow of a Revolutionary officer and barmaid at Hall's Corner Tavern in New York, is said to have decorated a drink with the feathers of roosters stolen from a loyalist neighbour. A group of French soldiers were served the drink and toasted Betsy with *'Vive le cock-tail'*.

Two further stories place the origins of the cocktail Mexico. One version has English sailors ashore at Campeche in Yucatan. A popular drink was a drac, a mixture of liquors stirred slowly with a wooden spoon. In one bar, the barman stirred the drinks not with a spoon, but with the root of a plant called cola de gallo – in English, a cock's tail. Rather than ask for dracs the English sailors took to asking for 'cock-tails'.

The second version was provided by Harry Craddock, the legendary bartender at the Savoy Hotel in London from 1920 to 1939. Craddock was the first president of the United Kingdom Bartender's Guild and was responsible for introducing the delights of the fashionable American cocktail to Europe. Americans touring Europe often referred to the bar at the Savoy as the '49th state' since it was the finest place to enjoy an American cocktail. In 1930 Craddock published the now highly collectable *Savoy Cocktail Book*. In Craddock's story, the cocktail was invented at the beginning of the 19th century when the American Army of the Southern States was fighting the forces of King Axolotl VIII of Mexico. When a truce was declared, the king offered the American general a drink. A sin-gle cup of liquor was brought in by the king's daughter who, realising that whoever drank first would offend the other, saved everyone's embarrassment by drinking it herself. The king's daughter just happened to be called Coctel and thus, her drink became 'cocktail'.

Modern masters

While all these stories offer an explanation of the origin of the word 'cocktail' few, if any, offer hints of what went into these remarkable drinks. The earliest mention of the ingredients of cocktails can be found in *The Balance and Columbian Repository*, a newspaper published in Hudson, New York, on 13 May 1806, which described the cocktail as 'a stimulating liquor composed of spirits of any kind, sugar, water, and bitters'.

The American barman 'Professor' Jerry Thomas was the first to produce a book of cocktail recipes in the 1860s, *The Bon Vivant's Guide, or How to Mix Drinks*. The 'Professor' became famous when he was the bartender at the Metropolitan Hotel in New York. Touring Europe, he travelled with a set of silver mixing cups from which he would trail a flame of liquid when he mixed his famous blue blazer cocktail.

The Professor's recipe book was soon followed by many others, but outstanding was Harry Johnson's *Illustrated Bartender's Manual*. Published in 1882, Johnson's book featured an illustration of an ice-filled bar glass with a metal cone – what was to become the modern cocktail shaker.

Today there are thousands of recipes for cocktails and mixed drinks. Some are simple, some elaborate. Some use only a few ingredients, others have so many ingredients that it's amazing they all fit into one glass! Everyone can make a good cocktail: there are no jealously guarded secrets, nor does it require years of toil. In this book you will find a good number of drinks that you can make straight away at home. You won't need to splash out on exotic liqueurs – not yet anyway!

All of the recipes in this book are based on gin, vodka, tequila, rum, brandy, whisky, vermouth, wine (including some champagne and fortified wines like sherry and port) with a few additions such as angostura bitters, grenadine, fruit juices and sparkling minerals. With a few ingredients, you should be able to make a fair proportion of the drinks on offer. A few, however, do use triple sec or a 'branded' ingredient such as Campari or Galliano and it is worthwhile investing in a bottle of each if you enjoy the flavour they impart. You will find more detailed information on each of the spirits in the section on ingredients and at the beginning of each chapter.

The recipes offered in this book are for you to try out for yourself. Choose a cocktail, a highball, a Rickey, a Collins, or a punch – or even a 'mocktail' – that catches your eye and try it. If it's too sweet for your taste, cut down on the sugar or liqueur content. If it's too sour, reduce the lemon or lime juice. Play around with the proportions until you find the 'perfect mix' and have fun!

Cocktail essentials

Many of the stock items you will need may be already in your kitchen cupboards or drinks cabinet. The job of making drinks is much easier – and more pleasurable – when everything is to hand. Consequently, whether the drinks are for an intimate 'dîner à deux', entertaining a few friends, a family get-together at Christmas or Thanksgiving, a summer barbecue or garden party or a more formal celebration, the most important thing is preparation. Lay everything out neatly and keep your utensils and glasses clean. Squeeze enough juice in advance, cut lemons, limes, oranges and other fruit for garnishes and twists and make sure that mixers and fruit juices are well chilled. Ask one or two friends to come around early – that way you can gossip and cut lemon slices at the same time.

Bar stock

The drinks in this book are for the most part based on a single base spirit (such as gin, vodka or rum) to which is added a second spirit, liqueur (either Cointreau or Galliano), bitters, juices or minerals. This way, you can choose your favourite spirit and create drinks around it. The exotically named, beautifully bottled and sometimes obscure liqueurs and spirits have been avoided. I leave these for you to discover and enjoy for yourself!

The most essential ingredient: ice, and lots of it!

Ice

You'll need ice – broken, crushed and cubes – and probably lots of it. Never use the same ice twice. Clean, clear ice cubes are hard to make, especially if you live in a hard-water area. Even bottled waters can make cloudy cubes. If your cubes are cloudy, you could use purified drinking water, available at your chemist, although it is more expensive than bottled. Alternatively, check out the ice on sale at your off license or liquor store. The cubes should be clear. If they're cloudy, you might as well save your money and make your own from tap water.

Keep ice cubes in an ice bucket and use tongs to pick them up. If they get stuck together, a quick squirt of soda water will separate them.

To make broken ice, place some cubes into a plastic bag and hit them with a rolling pin! The aim is to make each piece about one-third the original ice-cube size.

To make crushed ice, you could either carry on hitting the bag or else put the broken ice into a blender. Unless you have a heavy-duty blender, or one that the maker says will crush ice, don't put whole cubes in it. Your blades will never forgive you!

There are several ice crushers available on the market, both electric and manual. Remember, too, that broken and crushed ice will melt quickly, so make it just before you need it and use well-chilled glasses.

Base spirits

Choose the brand you enjoy most. Quality spirits may be a little more expensive, but a cocktail is no better than its poorest ingredient! The main base spirits are gin, vodka, rum (white and dark, see the section on rum, page 54), tequila, brandy and whisky.

For the sake of simplicity, when referring to whisky in this book, we have adopted the accepted British spelling of the word unless specifically referring to Irish or American whiskey, such as bourbon, rye, corn or Kentucky. Avoid using high-quality Scotch malt unless a recipe demands it. A good blend will be perfect.

Liqueurs

These are sweetish drinks made from a base spirit which is infused, macerated or redistilled with roots, barks, flowers, fruits or seeds. (In the United States, liqueurs are called cordials. In other English-speaking countries, however, a cordial is a non-alcoholic, concentrated fruit juice.) Some of the drinks in this book require Galliano, triple sec, such as Cointreau, and Campari

Galliano is a sweetish, gold-coloured liqueur from Lombardy in Italy and has a spicy, herbal taste tinged with vanilla. It comes in a very tall bottle and was named after Major Guiseppe Galliano, an Italian war hero from the Abyssinian Wars of 1895. The recipe, containing more than 80 herbs, roots, flowers and berries from Alpine regions, is a closely guarded secret and the method of

Cocktail shakers
come in many
shapes and
sizes

The corkscrew, an
essential bar tool.

production has remained unchanged since it was first made by the distiller Arturo Vaccari.

Triple sec

One of the most refined forms of Curaçao, triple sec a colourless liqueur made from the peel of small, green oranges native to the island of Curaçao in the Caribbean. Triple sec means ' triple dry', but the liqueur is not as dry as it sounds, and is a major ingredient in many of the most famous cocktails and mixed drinks. The world's best-known brand of triple sec is Cointreau, first made in 1849 at Angers, France, by brothers Edouard and Adolphe Cointreau. Curaçao can also come in different colours – blue, green, yellow and red – and is used mainly to produce many of the more vividly coloured modern cocktails and mixed drinks.

Campari really comes somewhere in between a bitters and a liqueur. It is a patent Italian aperitif (from the Latin *aperire*, 'to open', and thus an alcoholic drink taken before a meal to stimulate and sharpen the appetite). It is red and very dry, with a pronounced quinine taste, and can either be drunk 'on the rocks' with soda or used as the ingredient in a cocktail. Campari is the basis of two of the most famous cocktails, the Americano (page 186) and the Negroni (page 199).

Wines, aromatised wines and fortified wines

Vermouths are properly aromatised wines. The best-known French vermouth is Noilly Prat, made in Marseilles. It is very dry and is made with two white wines and 40 herbs which are steeped for 18 months. Turin, Italy, is the biggest vermouth-producing city and is the home of both Martini and Cinzano which produce excellent dry, extra dry and sweet vermouths, which can be either red or white.

Despite its red (Italian: *rosso*) colour, sweet vermouth is also made with white wine, albeit with sweeter grapes to which sweeteners, quinine and caramel are added.

Sherry and port

These two wonderful fortified wines are so often ignored or simply offered either 'straight' as an aperitif (in the case of sherry) or as a digestif (in the case of port). There are a number of delicious cocktails and mixed drinks which use these as their base and which offer an opportunity to be a little different. A good sherry choice for cocktails would be a fino, while for port, select a tawny. For more on these two wines, see pages 182–83.

Wines

Entire books have been written on the relative merits of individual wines. It really comes down to a simple matter of taste. The choice of wine or champagne is entirely up to you.

Beer

No matter what you have lovingly created, there will always be one person at the party who will want a beer – and nothing else. Take as much trouble with beer as you would with any spirit. Each has its own unique colour and flavour. Check out 'real ales' and those available from micro-breweries. Beer and ale are also the basis of some interesting cocktails and punches.

Stout is a very dark – almost black - ale and is used in a black velvet (page 189). Bitter amber ale is used in the punch called brown Betty (page 210).

Angostura bitters

In the recipes in this book you will frequently see in the ingredients '1 or 2 dashes bitters'. Bitters are an essential ingredient of a large number of cocktails. Oddly enough, bitters are bitter if you taste them straight, but their effect in a cocktail is almost the exact opposite. Bitters essences are alcoholic drinks made from roots, flowers, fruits and peels macerated in neutral spirit. The most famous patent bitters are angostura bitters

Originally made in the town of Angostura, (now Cuidad Bolivar), Venezuela, it is now produced in Trinidad. Angostura has over 40 ingredients, including gentian root and the bark from the cusparia tree. In this book, when you see bitters specified, use angostura bitters.

*Even though you will only add one or two dashes of angostura bitters to a drink, they do have an alcohol content of 45 per cent, so don't be tempted to add them to 'mocktails' (non-alcoholic drinks) for teetotallers, youngsters or 'designated drivers'.

Grenadine

Grenadine is a sweet syrup flavoured with pomegranate juice, which gives it its rich, rosy-pink colour. Prolonged exposure to the air once the bottle has been opened will make the syrup ferment and mould, so keep an eye on it. To stop the fermentation, you could add about 10 per cent vodka – but remember, your grenadine should not then be used in mocktails! You could perhaps decant some grenadine into another bottle, add vodka to 10 per cent of the volume, label it and keep the remainder as 'unadulterated'. Keep the grenadine in a cool place, but don't refrigerate it as this can cause the sugar to crystallise, or at least harden, which prevents it from mixing easily with other drinks.

Minerals and juices

If you've purchased a good-quality spirit, why spoil it with poor-quality minerals and juices? Squeeze your own citrus juices or buy the best you can find and serve chilled. A comprehensive selection includes: soda water, cola, tonic water, ginger ale, lemonade, lemon-lime soda (such as 7-Up), tomato juice, cranberry juice, grape juice, pineapple juice, orange juice, apple juice, grapefruit juice, lemon juice, lime juice and Rose's Lime Juice. it is also worth trying some of the more 'exotic' juices, such as passionfruit, mango, peach and tangerine

This handy little gadget makes zest from citrus fruit and can also be used to make twists and spirals.

Fresh fruit

Freshly squeezed citrus fruits will produce the best juice. Citrus fruits other than lemons turn soft and show spots as they age, while lemons turn hard. While the flesh inside might be OK, it may have an peculiar taste. Choose fruits with bright skins and remember to wash them before using the skin for twists. Once squeezed, fruit juices will slowly start to ferment. Refrigeration will slow the process, but my advice is 'buy 'em fresh, squeeze 'em fresh and use 'em fresh'.

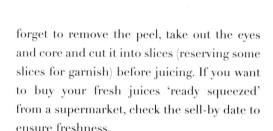

Strain lemon and lime juice before use to ensure no pips get in the drink. Likewise, you might want to strain other citrus juices. Strain through a fine nylon sieve to ensure that clear drinks remain unclouded by the juice. If you don't have the energy or time to hand-squeeze your fruit and don't have one of those fancy electric juicers, try using a mixer/blender. Peel the fruit (reserving the peel), pulp it at high speed and strain. Peaches and mangos can be 'squeezed' in a blender – and yes, you can even do a pineapple this way, but don't forget to remove the peel, take out the eyes and core and cut it into slices (reserving some slices for garnish) before juicing. If you want to buy your fresh juices 'ready squeezed' from a supermarket, check the sell-by date to ensure freshness.

Although there are many famous and delicious cocktails which use cream or milk, none are included in this book. Yoghurt, however, is a wonderful ingredient in mocktails, and you will find a few 'healthy options' to try in that section.

The famous pina colada, possibly the most popular cocktail in the world, does use coconut cream as one of its ingredients. This is very simple to make and the instructions are given alongside the recipe (see page 73).

Some bartenders also use a teaspoon of raw egg white or egg yolk to give a cocktail a 'silver' and 'frothy' or 'golden' finish. Although the egg cannot be tasted, many people don't like the idea of raw egg in their drink. Furthermore, some people may be advised on medical grounds to avoid raw eggs altogether. In this book, drinks that include egg are omitted.

Condiments

Drinks with tomato juice, such as the bloody Mary (page 82) can be 'spiced up' according to taste with Worcestershire sauce*, Tabasco sauce, ground black pepper and perhaps a few celery seeds.

* Vegetarians should note that one of the ingredients of Worcestershire sauce is anchovy essence and they may prefer to avoid this.

You will also need

Salt preferably coarsely ground, if you want to make the tequila-based Margarita (page 142) or the vodka-based salty dog (page 101).

Sugar in cube form; granulated sugar and castor sugar (sometimes called 'superfine' in recipe books). Gomme syrup is simply a sugar syrup and is easy to make. The object is to make the sugar syrup as heavy as possible without crystallisation. Gomme syrup is used in place of castor sugar and most bartenders prefer it since there is less risk of there being

a sediment at the bottom of the glass and it also saves time.

Spices these are used particularly in punches and hot drinks. Nutmeg, ginger, cinnamon and cloves are probably already in your kitchen cupboard.

Garnishes: green cocktail olives, cocktail onions, sprigs of fresh mint. Mint is an easy plant to grow in a garden or on a window sill.

There are many varieties, including pineapple mint, apple mint and variegated (with yellow and green leaves) varieties. Grow mint in a pot even in the garden – that is unless you want your garden full of it as it will spread and overwhelm other plants.

Wedges, slices and twists of orange, lemon slices and lime slices; pineapple and grapefruit slices, maraschino cherries are also useful. Seasonal fruit is always an attractive and delicious garnish for mocktails and party punches: try cool cucumber or apple wedges.

When you see the term 'garnish with lemon twist',

follow these steps:

1. Hold the peel, coloured side down, over the top of the drink.
2. Twist the peel. This releases the volatile oil into the drink.
3. Rub the coloured side of the peel along the rim of the glass and then discard the peel, unless otherwise stated. If, however, you find you like the bitter sharpness of the citrus oil, you can drop the twist into the drink.

To make gomme syrup:

Add three cups of granulated sugar to one cup of cold water. Bring to the boil and reduce the heat. Allow to simmer for two minutes. Skim the surface and allow to cool. Then pour off into a bottle and store in a cool place. Don't keep it in the fridge as the sugar may crystallise.

To make orange/lemon/lime slices:

1. Cut the 'knobs' off the top and tail of the fruit. Cut deep enough to expose the pulp.
2. Cut the orange in half lengthways from top to tail.
3. Put each orange half cut side down and cut crosswise into ¼ inch-thick slices.
4 Cut into the centre of each slice – start at the flat fruit edge and go just up to, but not into, the peel.
5. Slip the cut onto the rim of the glass so that it hangs half-in, half-out.

Preparing garnishes

Don't just slice fruit – try cutting citrus peel into shapes such as stars, crescents or hearts, that can be speared on a cocktail stick and used to decorate drinks. Remember to wash the fruit before you use it.

To make wedges:

1. Cut the 'knobs' off the top and tail of the fruit.
2. Slice the fruit in half from top to bottom, and then again across the 'equator'.
3. Cut each piece into four equal wedges.
4. When you squeeze a wedge, hold it over the glass and squeeze it downwards into the drink. Try shielding the glass with your other hand: by some unexplained phenomenon of physics, lemon juice will always hit you in the eye! Drop the wedge into the drink.

To make twists:

Twists are usually made of lemon, but sometimes limes and oranges are used.

1. Cut a slice from the top and tail of the fruit – just thick enough to expose the pulp.
2. Using a sharp knife, cut through the peel into the fruit from top to tail.
3. Insert a small spoon through the cut. The idea is to separate the fruit from the peel: work the spoon up and down and around the inside of the peel.
4. Once the fruit is separated from the peel, take it out and use it for juice.
5. Cut the peel into thin strips – as thin as possible – cutting lengthways from top to tail.

Gadgets & gizmos

In many books and bartender's guides, the lists of 'necessary equipment' can be off-putting. Once again, you will probably already have some items, such as a sharp paring knife, a strainer, and a can and bottle opener. Most of the specially designed 'gadgets' that are the tools of the trade are widely available in kitchen shops and department stores. The following items are really essential for mixing drinks and cocktails.

Shaker This is fundamental tool of the cocktail bartender. A shaker is used in making drinks that contain fruit juices, syrups, thick liqueurs or any ingredients that need a thorough mix. Because the ice gets shaken about, there will be some dilution and clear drinks cannot easily be produced.

The capacity of the shaker should be enough to hold two drinks and ice – around 400g (14 oz) or so. There are two types of shaker to choose from.

The assembled shaker and its component parts, showing the built-in strainer.

The familiar stainless-steel shaker has a strainer built into the lid and a cap which doubles as a measure – usually around 60g(2 oz). It is essential that the shaker does not leak from the main seal when pouring into the glass. If it does develop a drip, wrap a cloth around the seal when you shake.

The second type of shaker is the Boston shaker (sometimes called an American shaker). The Boston shaker has one glass flat-bottomed cone which slots into larger steel flat-bottomed cone. When you shake, make sure that the metal half is on the bottom. While a Boston shaker is easier to 'break open', it can be harder to pour and you will need a strainer.

Hawthorn strainer A stray piece of ice or a lemon pip entering a drink will spoil its taste and look. A Hawthorn strainer is the classic bartender's model. The name of the maker, Hawthorn, is spelled out in strainer holes and around the edge is a coil which fits neatly in the glass cone of the Boston shaker. You have to hold the Hawthorn tightly in place with your fingers, which can be tricky at first. If you prefer, look for a strainer that clips onto the rim of the mixing glass.

Paring knife As sharp as possible. Keep it sharp and keep it safe.

Cutting board This doesn't have to be big or elaborate. You'll need it for cutting citrus slices, twists and decorative spirals of peel.

Lemon squeezer This can be any style or the style that you are most comfortable with. The traditional glass citrus reamer – with the raised dome in the middle of a bowl – is fine, but I recommend passing the juice through a fine nylon sieve to remove pips and stray 'teardrops' of fruit pulp. If you've invited a number of guests for drinks, you'll have to squeeze plenty of juice in advance.

Mixing glass This glass is used for mixing most drinks that don't have fruit juices – drinks that are clear, not cloudy. Use a mixing glass with a pouring spout to stop the ice from falling into the drinking glass when you pour. A mixing glass should hold around 16 oz of liquid. (See also glass pitcher/jug.)

Jigger America and Britain each have their own ideas about what constitutes a 'fluid ounce'. Continental Europe prefers metric measurements in centilitre/millilitre form. The 'classic' jigger, the little metal measuring cup, that is used in bars in the United States measures 1 1/2 US oz. The measure in a British jigger (1 imperial oz) contains 0.96 US fluid oz. In effect, there's little very little difference: 1 imperial fl oz = 28.4 ml and 1 US fl oz = 29.6 ml. The recipes in this book use the term measure and assumes 1 measure = 25 ml.

Confused? Don't worry!

It doesn't matter how big the 'jigger' is, just as long as you use the same measure throughout the recipe. You could use a shot glass (these measure about 2 fl oz or 57 ml), the measure on top of your shaker; or you could splash out on your own personal set. A useful tip, however, is to see how many measures (use water to test!) will fit into each glass and adjust the quantities to fit the glass exactly.

Soon you will be able to judge by eye, and tasting will help you to add more or less of an ingredient to achieve the perfect mix.

Measuring spoons Two teaspoons are helpful, one for dry substances and one for liquids. A tablespoon is also useful. All measures are level spoons unless otherwise stated.

Ice bucket Size and insulation are important. Don't be tempted by a pleasing design if it doesn't function well.

Tongs Tongs are better than an ice scoop: shaking and mixing with ice will dilute drinks sufficiently without adding a scoop of melted ice water as well! Use a scoop, or even a slotted spoon, for crushed ice.

Long-handled bar spoon This is a long, flat-headed spoon with a twisted shaft that is used to stir drinks in a mixing glass. An ordinary long-handled spoon works just as well.

Muddler Muddlers come in various shapes and sizes. Large ones are used with the mixing glass, smaller ones are for the drinkers to fiddle with. They have a 'bulb' at the end and are intended to crush sugar or pound mint in a drink. You could use a mortar and pestle for crushing mint for your mint julep (page 117) or a long-handled wooden spoon in the mixing glass/pitcher. As long as it reaches the bottom, it will do and it won't scratch.

Swizzlers Similar to a muddler, but with a 'paddle' on the end. You place the shaft between the palms of your hand and rub them together so that the paddle agitates the drink. Like muddlers, swizzle sticks are often used simply for decoration.

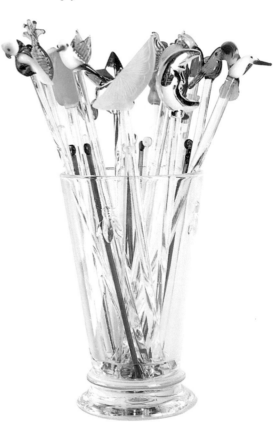

Glass pitcher/jug For iced water or fruit juices. Choose one with an involuted pourer (a turned-over lip). This will keep back the ice cubes and you can use it instead of a mixing glass.

Glass-cleaning cloth You need a glass cloth to keep your glassware sparkling and free from the bits of lint that ordinary 'linens' leave behind. They're easy to spot – they have the word 'Glass' woven into them.

Corkscrew Go for the Bartender's Friend, an all-in-one opener for corked and crown-topped bottles, as well as cans.

Cocktail sticks Wooden and coloured plastic ones are readily available.

Straws Long and short, bendy and straight, plain and striped, a good variety is more fun.

Napkins and coasters Somewhere to place the cocktail stick after you've eaten the garnish.

Paper parasols Why not? Decoration is a personal thing, but a cocktail should be pleasing to the eye, as well as to the palate. Some diehards do, however, think that the only good decoration is an edible one.

Blender/food processor Although not essential, a blender or food processor is ideal for making juices and frozen daiquiris. You can also make many other 'shaken' cocktails in a blender and they are particularly useful if you are making a large number of the same drinks for a party.

Glassware

All glasses must be spotless! After washing, polish them completely dry with a clean glass cloth to avoid stains. A beautiful glass will give maximum visual impact. There are, naturally, 'classic' glasses for particular drinks, but there are infinite designs to choose from. Nevertheless it's worth looking for glasses with a fine rim; a slender stem (when appropriate), long enough so that the cool drink is not warmed by the hand's heat; a glass that suits the drink it will hold – the right size and the right shape, and, if necessary, heat-proof for hot toddies. The recipes in this book advise you which type of glass to use. Useful glasses include the following.

Cocktail glass Elegant and essential, around 120-150ml (4–5 fl oz), with a stem long enough to protect the bowl from the heat of the hand and the opening wide enough to display a garnish.

Old fashioned Also called a rocks glass This is used for any cocktails served 'on the rocks'; 170-230g (6-8 oz) capacity is a good size.

Highball This is a tallish glass, between 230-280g (8-10 oz). A useful glass, it can serve many purposes.

Collins This is for long drinks – the taller the better. Collins glasses, unlike highballs, always have perfectly straight sides. Around 280-380g (10-12 oz) capacity.

Sour This is a stemmed glass which is used for drinks that aren't strictly cocktails, but aren't 'long' either. A good-looking 'white-wine glass' will do very well.

Ballon A 'balloon' is basically a red-wine glass, of 240-300ml (8–10fl oz) capacity. Choose a well-rounded ballon with plenty of room for ice and garnish. Coloured drinks look particularly attractive in these glasses. A large ballon can be used as a goblet.

Champagne saucer and champagne flute

The traditional champagne saucer (said to have been modelled on Marie-Antoinette's bosom) was used when Madeira cake was dunked in the champagne. Although elegant and unmistakable, the open saucer shape lets the bubbles dissipate quickly. Nevertheless, some cocktails are traditionally served in a champagne saucer. Champagne flutes are stemmed, narrow, tulip-shaped glasses. Not only do they look pleasing, flutes also retain the bubbles in a drink for longer. But not even a flute will protect a sparkling drink from the ravages of lipstick. It may look glamorous, but the chemicals in the 'lippie' make fizzy drinks (beer included) loose their sparkle.

Toddy For hot drinks you'll need heat-proof glasses with handles.

Glasses need to be chilled, ready to receive the drink (except for toddies, which should be warm). There are a number of ways to chill glasses. Either put them in the freezer for 20 to 30 minutes. (Warning: Don't put crystal glasses in the freezer! They may shatter) or place an ice cube in the bottom of the glass, swirl it around and discard.

To really give a glass a good, frosted look, fill each glass with crushed ice and put it in the refrigerator. Throw away the crushed ice just before the drink is poured in.

Some drinks, like Margaritas, have a frosted effect on the rims. This is done with either sugar or salt (depending on the drink). Dampen the rim of the pre-chilled glass with a slice of lemon (or lime) and dip the rim into a saucer of castor sugar or salt. Remember to pick up glasses by the stems or by the bottom of the glass so the frost is not disturbed or the glass marked by finger prints.

Cocktail terminology

BUILD Pour the ingredients directly into the drinking glass.
DASH A tiny amount, a drop.
GARNISH Decorate or attach to the rim of the glass.
LONG A drink with five measures or more of liquid.
MUDDLE Mashing or grinding herbs, such as mint, into a smooth paste in the bottom of a glass.
ON THE ROCKS Poured over ice.
SHAKE In a cocktail shaker, shake for 8 to 10 seconds: the whole shaker should feel cold.

SHORT Less than five measures of liquid before shaking.
STRAIGHT UP Mixed and served without ice.
STRAIN Pour out, leaving behind the ice and any other solids.
SHOOTER A short drink, usually downed 'in one'.
TWIST 1–2 inches (3–6 cm) length of pith-free citrus peel, held 'skin side' over a drink and twisted in the middle to release the essential oil. The peel is usually discarded but can, if preferred, be dropped in the drink.

Dos and don'ts

Do get into the habit of adding the cheapest ingredients – such as juices – first to the shaker or mixing glass. If you make a mistake, you won't have wasted too much valuable spirit.

Do serve drinks with a mixer in a highball glass. Fill the glass two-thirds full with ice and add the ingredients.

Do use a mixing glass for cocktails containing only alcoholic products.

Do shake sharply for about 8 to 10 seconds.

Do serve cocktails immediately. If you leave them to stand they will separate.

Do wash the shaker or mixing glass after each 'batch'. Sugar/syrup needs attention as it will make the join in the shaker sticky.

Don't shake fizzy drinks!

Don't use ice cubes twice. Always use clean ice.

Don't add alcoholic bitters or syrups to non-alcoholic mocktails.

Don't force an alcoholic drink on anyone. Offer a mocktail instead.

Don't forget that the volume of a drink mixed with ice will increase. Make sure the glass is large enough to hold it.

Don't forget the teetotallers and drivers. Do not encourage under-age drinking, drink-driving, drunkenness, or anti-social behaviour.

Remember

Cocktails and mixed drinks are delicious, and they are alcoholic. If you're thirsty, drink water or juice. A cocktail is for sipping and enjoying with friends. Think of American humorist and playwright George Ade's words from his play *The Sultan of Sula* (1903):

R-E-M-O-R-S-E!

Those dry Martinis did the work for me;

Last night at twelve I felt immense,

Today I feel like thirty cents.

Gin cocktails

martini
see page 48.

The word gin is believed to have come about from the mispronunciation of foreign names for the juniper berry from which the liquor is distilled. Some believe that the word gin is derived from the Dutch word *jenever*: Dr Sylvius de la Boe first formulated the liquor as a treatment for kidney complaints at the university medical school in Leyden in the mid-16th century. Others say that it comes from the French word *genièvre*, while a few maintain that it was Italy that gave us *ginepro*, since Tuscany continues to be the main producer of the juniper berries which give gin its perfume and taste.

Gin became widely popular in Britain in the 17th century when the Dutch William III (who married Mary II and became king of England in 1689) raised the excise duties on French wines and brandies as a measure of revenge for French hostilities in Holland. Gin's comparatively low cost, coupled with its potency, meant that it soon found its way into most people's lives and into popular culture. By the 18th century gin was the 'poor man's tea' (tea was so expensive that it was kept under lock and key in specially designed caddies). Soldiers drank gin before battle to give them 'Dutch courage'; juniper berries were falsely believed to induce miscarriages and gin became known as 'mother's ruin'.

By the 1740s, gin consumption had reached 20 million gallons annually. Sale was virtually unrestricted, so anyone could set up a still and open a gin shop.

Advertisements promised 'Drunk for a penny. Dead drunk for tuppence'. Contemporaries estimated that there was one gin shop for every six houses in London. The Gin Act of 1736 was an attempt by Parliament to limit the appalling scenes of public drunkenness as portrayed in Hogarth's famous engraving *Gin Lane* (1751) and to curb the rising mortality rate. Distillers were taxed, but the act was impossible to enforce and illegal stills remained widespread. It was only by passing a series of laws that imposed restrictions on public houses and the sale of gin that some measure of sobriety was restored.

In the 20th century, during Prohibition in America (1919–33), the alternative to expensive smuggled, bootlegged spirits was an illicit still. By 1929 there were more than a hundred recipes for 'bathtub' gin and hundreds more recipes for cocktails to disguise the taste!

Today's gin is made by infusing juniper berries and other flavourings into a high-quality, neutral grain spirit, usually corn, malted barley and sometimes a small amount of another grain. Coriander is a flavouring (known as a botanical) in both Dutch jenevers and London Dry gin. London Dry gin is a style of gin: it can be made anywhere as long as the base spirit is rectified to neutrality before being redistilled with the botanical flavourings. Dutch jenevers, in contrast, retain the flavour of the grain in the spirit. Plymouth gin is made in only in Plymouth, Devon, with the natural water from Dartmoor. It was apparently the Royal Navy who first mixed gin with angostura bitters to make a 'pink gin', which, even today, is still properly made with Plymouth gin.

pink pussycat
see page 51.

method:	SHAKER
glass:	COCKTAIL

Bennet cocktail

This lime-flavour cocktail was invented in the 1920s.
Originally it was served 'straight up' without the sugar. It is also
sometimes served in an old-fashioned glass filled with broken ice.
Try the variations for yourself.

Ingredients:

ice cubes

2 measures gin

⅔ measure lime juice

⅓ measure sugar syrup

I dash bitters

Gin

Method:

Half-fill the shaker with ice
cubes.
Add the gin, lime juice, sugar
syrup and bitters.
Shake and strain into a
cocktail glass.

Bernardo

A delicious and sophisticated drink – ideal for unwinding after a long day!

Ingredients:

ice cubes

2 measures gin

½ measure triple sec or Cointreau

2 teaspoons lemon juice

2 dashes bitters

1 lemon twist

Gin

Method:

Half-fill the shaker with ice cubes.

Add the gin, Cointreau, lemon juice and bitters.

Shake well and then strain into a cocktail glass.

Garnish with the lemon twist.

method:	SHAKER
glass:	COCKTAIL

Bronx cocktail

This cocktail was devised in 1906 by Johnny Solon, the celebrated barman at the Waldorf Astoria Hotel in New York. Johnny was apparently inspired following a trip to the Bronx Zoo. Originally served straight up in a cocktail glass, it's just as nice in an old-fashioned glass three-quarters filled with broken ice.

Ingredients:

ice cubes
1½ measures gin
¾ measure rosso vermouth
¾ measure dry vermouth
¾ measure orange juice

Gin

Method:

Half-fill the shaker with ice cubes.
Add the gin, two ver-mouths and the orange juice and shake well.
Strain into a cocktail glass.

Variations:

Bloody Bronx

use blood orange juice.

Dry Bronx

replace the sweet, rosso vermouth with dry (1½ measures dry vermouth in total).

Captain's table

This cocktail includes Campari, Italy's most famous aperitif.

Ingredients:

ice cubes

2 measures gin

½ measure Campari

1 teaspoon grenadine

1 measure orange juice

4 measures ginger ale

1 maraschino cherry

Gin

Method:

Half-fill the shaker with ice cubes.

Add the gin, Campari, grenadine and orange juice. Shake well and strain into a highball glass almost filled with ice cubes.

Top up with the ginger ale and garnish with the cherry.

method: SHAKER

glass: COCKTAIL

Crimson sunset

Tastes wonderful and looks lovely – but it may require a little practice!

Ingredients:

ice cubes

2 measures gin

½ measures tawny port

2 teaspoons lemon juice

½ teaspoon grenadine

Gin

Method:

Half-fill the shaker with ice cubes.

Add the gin and lemon juice only and shake well.

Strain into a cocktail glass.

Drop the grenadine into the centre of the drink and float the port on top.

The Collins

The tallest of the mixed drinks, the original Collins was, in fact, John Collins.
He was a well-known head waiter at Limmer's, a popular coffee house and hotel in
London's Conduit Street between 1790 and 1817. His original recipe called for Dutch
jenever and never really caught on until someone used Old Tom
gin and the Tom Collins was born.

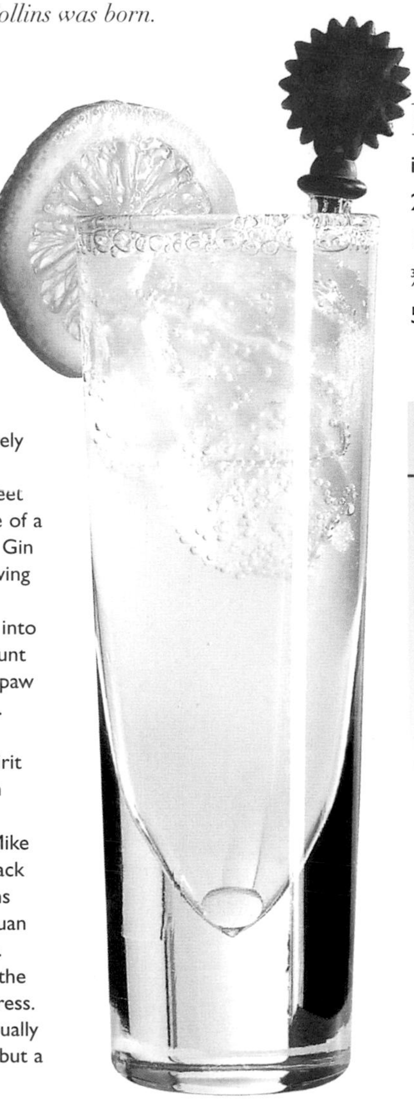

Ingredients:

ice cubes
2 measures gin
1 measure lemon juice
¾ measure sugar syrup
5 measure soda water

Gin

Method:

Fill a frosted glass two-thirds full with ice, add the lemon juice, sugar syrup and gin. Top with soda water and stir. Garnish with lemon slice and serve with straws.

Old Tom gin is a sweet gin, now rarely produced, and was supposedly first distilled by Captain Dudley Bradstreet in London in 1738. Taking advantage of a loophole in the prohibitionist 1736 Gin Act, Bradstreet used a wooden carving of a tom cat as his shop sign. Customers placed a sum of money into the mouth and an appropriate amount of gin would be dispensed from its paw – via a tube – into the buyer's glass. Now a Tom Collins is made with London gin, but you can use any spirit of your choice. In America, the John Collins lives on and is made with bourbon or whisky, while cousins Mike Collins (made with Irish whiskey), Jack Collins (apple brandy), Pierre Collins (cognac), Pedro Collins (rum) and Juan Collins (tequila) make up the family. Sadly, all the relatives are male and the only Joan Collins is the popular actress. Whatever spirit is used, they are usually served in their own Collins glass – but a highball is just fine.

method:	MIXING GLASS
glass:	COCKTAIL
garnish:	LEMON TWIST

Delmonico cocktail

A classy cocktail for a relaxing evening.

Ingredients:

ice cubes

1 measure gin

½ measure brandy

½ measure sweet vermouth

½ measure dry vermouth

1 dash angostura bitters

1 lemon twist

Gin

Method:

Half-fill a mixing glass with
ice cubes.

Add the gin, brandy, two
vermouths and the bitters.
Stir well and strain into a
cocktail glass.

Garnish with the lemon
twist.

Variations:

If you use orange bitters in
place of angostura, you will
make a Harvard.

Dragonfly

*A very simple drink to mix and a refreshing
change from the usual 'gin and tonic'.*

Ingredients:

ice cubes
½ measures gin
4 measures ginger ale
1 lime wedge

Gin

Method:

Fill a highball glass almost to
the top with ice cubes.
Add the gin and the ginger
ale and then garnish with the
wedge of lime.

method:	MIXING GLASS
glass:	COCKTAIL
garnish:	COCKTAIL OLIVE

Fifty-fifty

An easy recipe to remember, but a drink not easily forgotten.

Ingredients:

ice cubes

1½ measures gin

1½ measures dry vermouth

1 cocktail olive

Gin

Method:

Half-fill the mixing glass with ice cubes.

Add the gin and vermouth.

Stir well and strain into a cocktail glass.

Garnish with the olive.

Flying Dutchman

*The name of this drink probably stems from the fact
that it was made with Dutch jenever and triple sec, the
orange liqueur Curaçao from the island of the same
name in the former Dutch West Indies.*

Ingredients:

ice cubes

2 measures gin

½ measure triple sec or Cointreau

Gin

Method:

Almost fill an old-fashioned
glass with ice cubes.
Add the gin and the
Cointreau and stir well.

method:	BUILD
glass:	OLD FASHIONED

Gentlemen's club

This is the ideal drink for any man who thinks cocktails are for girls!

Ingredients:

ice cubes

1½ measures gin

1 measure brandy

1 measure sweet vermouth

1 measure club soda

Gin

Method:

Almost fill an old-fashioned glass with ice cubes.
Add the gin, brandy and vermouth.
Add the soda and stir well.

Gibson

*This variation on the dry Martini was created at the
Player's Club in New York in the 1940s for the American
artist and illustrator Charles Dana Gibson. One story has it that
Gibson didn't like olives, so asked for a cocktail onion instead. The
barman, thinking of the shapely 'Gibson Girls' the illustrator had
made famous, added two onions in their honour!*

Ingredients:

ice cubes
2½ measures gin
1½ teaspoons dry vermouth
2 cocktail onions

Gin

Method:

Half-fill the mixing glass with
ice cubes.
Add the gin and vermouth.
Stir well and strain into a
cocktail glass.
Add the two cocktail onions.

method:	BUILD
glass:	OLD FASHIONED
garnish:	WEDGE OF LIME

Gimlet

A gimlet is a small, pointed hand tool used to bore holes in wood. They were often used in bars to tap into barrels, and soon the word gimlet came to mean a small, sharp cocktail. Gimlets seem to have been concocted originally by British residents in the Far East after the First World War. Gin and lime juice are the two ingredients. Some say that freshly squeezed lime juice was used, but others believe that Rose's Lime Juice, which is concentrated and sweetened, was preferred. Although limes were probably plentiful, the British may well have used the cordial since it predates the gimlet recipes.

Ingredients:

ice cubes
2 measures gin (some insist on
Plymouth gin)
¾ measure Rose's Lime Juice
1 measure cold soda water
(optional)

Gin

Method:

Pour the gin and the
lime cordial into an old-
fashioned glass filled with
ice and stir.
Add the soda (if desired) and
garnish with the lime wedge.

Variations:

Rum, tequila or vodka can
replace the gin if you prefer.
Whatever the spirit, lime
juice cordial is the 'correct'
accompaniment.

Gin daisy

'Daisies' were invented in America and have been around since the 1850s. Originally they were served in a tankard and straight up, but today an old-fashioned glass with plenty of broken or crushed ice is more usual. A small amount of fruit syrup is always used and can be complemented by using a little seasonal fruit as garnish. If any soda is added, it should never be more than half the quantity of the spirit.

Ingredients:

ice cubes

broken ice

2 measures gin

1 measure lemon juice

½ level teaspoon castor sugar

1 teaspoon grenadine

1 measure soda water
(optional)

1 maraschino cherry

1 orange slice

1 sprig mint

Gin

Method:

Half-fill the shaker with ice cubes.

Add the gin, lemon juice, sugar and grenadine.

Shake well and strain into an old-fashioned glass filled with broken ice.

Top up with soda if desired.

Garnish with the cherry and orange slice.

Variations:

Any spirit base can be used to make a daisy. Try substituting the gin with brandy or vodka. For a rum daisy, leave out the sugar and use 1½ measure white rum, 1 measure lime juice, 1 teaspoon grenadine and garnish with twists of lime and orange. See also the golden daisy (page 114).

Gin fizz

The fizz was first mentioned in the 1870s, and although it is similar to the Collins, a fizz is always shaken before adding the soda and was traditionally served at around 11.30 am. Whatever time you prefer your drink, a fizz should be served immediately after preparation. Beware ordering some of the beautifully named fizzes in a bar, as some classic recipes use raw egg to give more froth at the finish. If you're not happy with the idea of egg in your drink, let the barman know.

Ingredients:

ice cubes
2 measures gin
1 measure lemon juice
1 teaspoon castor sugar
(or 1 dash of gomme syrup)
5 measures soda water –
preferably dispensed from a
soda siphon, but still very
chilled!

Gin

Method:

Half-fill the shaker with ice cubes.
Add the gin, sugar and lemon juice and shake as hard as you can. (Alternatively, use crushed ice and an electric blender.)
Strain into a frosted highball glass half-filled with ice.
Add the soda while simultaneously stirring with a swizzle stick or muddler.
Drink immediately through a straw while the fizz fizzes!

Gin Rickey

A close cousin of the fizz and the Collins, the Rickey contains no sugar, however. The cocktail of gin, lime juice and soda water was first made in around 1893 in Shoemakers Restaurant in Washington, DC, for a Congressional lobbyist from Kentucky, Joe 'Colonel Jim' Rickey.

Ingredients:

ice cubes
2 measures gin
juice of 1 lime
4 measures soda water

Variations:

A Rickey can be made using any spirit as its base: replace the gin with 2 measures of either bourbon, brandy, rum or vodka.

Gin

Method:

Into a highball glass half-filled with ice, squeeze the juice of the lime.
Add the gin and stir.
Add the soda water and garnish with the wedge of lime. (Alternatively, drop half of the spent lime shell into the glass after squeezing!)

method:	SHAKER
glass:	HIGHBALL
garnish:	TWIST OF LEMON, SPRINKLING OF NUTMEG (OPTIONAL)

Gin sling

The sling first appeared in literature as far back as 1759 and appears to have been derived from the German word schlingen, *which means 'to swallow quickly'. However, a sling, like a gimlet, is also a bar tool, and was used to handle barrels. Slings are sweetish, long drinks traditionally based on gin and sometimes topped with plain water rather than soda. A true sling should contain lemon or lime juice and sugar/syrup or a sweet liqueur. The Singapore sling, created in 1915 by Ngiam Tong Boon at the Raffles Hotel in Singapore, contains cherry brandy. The basic gin sling, as given in Harry Craddock's 'cocktail bible',* The Savoy Cocktail Book *contains only the base spirit, sugar, water and one lump of ice.*

Ingredients:

ice cubes
2 measures gin
1 measure lemon juice
⅔ measure gomme syrup
2 measures cold water
nutmeg (optional)

Gin

Method:

Half-fill the shaker with ice cubes.
Add the gin, gomme syrup, lemon juice and water and shake well.
Strain into highball glass almost filled with ice cubes.
Garnish with the lemon twist.
Sprinkle with nutmeg (optional).

Variations:

Any base spirit and any fruit juice can be used to make a sling. Experiment by replacing the gin with either bourbon, brandy, rum, Scotch or vodka.

Gin swizzle

Swizzles were devised in the West Indies and first became popular with travellers in the early years of the 19th century. Originally, swizzles were made with rum, lime juice, gomme syrup or a liqueur, crushed ice and sometimes soda water. Other ingredients, such as fruit juices, were added in small quantities to add subtle colour or flavour. Swizzling the drink gives it a foamy appearance and frosts the glass. A great party drink, you can make swizzles in a pitcher, pour into chilled glasses and decorate with sprigs of mint.

Ingredients:

ice cubes
2 measures gin
1½ measures lime juice
1 teaspoon castor sugar
1 dash bitters
2–3 measures soda water

Variations:

To make up a pitcher of gin swizzles, fill the pitcher two-thirds full with crushed ice and add the ingredients. Give the mix a good, hard swizzle – put the stick between the flat palms of your hand and rub them together – until the pitcher is frosted. Pour into chilled glasses, add a swizzle stick, straws and garnish.

Any spirit can be used to make a swizzle. Lime juice works best with gin or rum, while lemon juice works best with other spirits.

Gin

Method:

Half-fill the shaker with ice cubes.
Add the lime juice, gin, sugar and bitters and shake well. Almost fill a Collins glass with ice cubes and then stir them with a swizzle stick until the glass is frosted. Strain the mixture in the shaker into the glass and add the soda. Serve with a swizzle stick and straws.

method:	SHAKER
glass:	OLD FASHIONED
garnish:	PINEAPPLE SLICE

Grass skirt

A Polynesian kingdom from the 6th century until 1893, Hawaii became a republic in 1894 and a United States territory in 1900 before becoming a state in 1959. The beautiful islands not only provide its most famous fruit, the pineapple, but hundreds of species of flowers that grow nowhere else in the world. As for the people, Richard Henry Dana Jnr wrote in
Two Years Before the Mast *(1840):*
'I would have trusted my life and my fortune in the hands of any one of these people;...had I wished for a favor or act of sacrifice, I would have gone to them all, in turn, before I should have applied to one of my own countrymen...'

Ingredients:

ice cubes
1½ measures gin
1 measure triple sec or
Cointreau
1 measure pineapple juice
½ teaspoon grenadine
1 pineapple slice

Gin

Method:

Half-fill the shaker with ice cubes.
Add the gin, triple sec or Cointreau, pineapple juice and grenadine.
Shake well and pour unstrained into an old-fashioned glass and garnish with the pineapple slice.

Honolulu cocktail

This recipe was devised by Victor Bergeron, better known as 'Trader' Vic. In the 1930s he opened a bar called Hinky Dinks in Oakland, California. The bar originally had a 'hunting and shooting' theme, but this was soon changed to a Pacific Island theme. Trader Vic's combination of exotic food and 'tropical' drinks, such as Dr Funk of Tahiti, the suffering bastard and the white witch, soon brought him fame, and today there are a number of his restaurants around the world.

Gin

Ingredients:

ice cubes

1½ measures gin

½ teaspoon castor sugar

¼ teaspoon orange juice

¼ teaspoon pineapple juice

¼ teaspoon lemon juice

1 dash bitters

Method:

Half-fill the shaker with ice cubes.

Add the gin, sugar, orange, lemon and pineapple juice and the bitter.

Shake well and then strain into a well-chilled cocktail glass.

method:	MIXING GLASS
glass:	COCKTAIL – THOROUGHLY CHILLED
garnish:	A GREEN OLIVE (BUT NEVER, EVER A STUFFED OLIVE) OR A TWIST OF LEMON (TO BE DISCARDED)

Martini

'Let's get out of these wet clothes and into a dry Martini'.
So goes the line in the 1937 film Every Day's a Holiday, *starring Mae West. The undoubted king of cocktails, the drink of the rich, glamorous and the famous, the Martini has a long history, which, like the recipe for the 'perfect' or the 'driest' dry Martini, continues to be hotly debated. Some say the Martini was invented for John D Rockefeller by a bartender called Martini di Arma di Taggia at the Knickerbocker Hotel in New York in 1910. In Martinez, California, about 32km (20 miles) from San Francisco, a bronze plaque announces that in 1874, bartender Julio Richelieu created the Martinez Special. A couple of drinks later, the 'z' got lost! For more on the legend, lore, and lure of the Martini, read Barnaby Conrad III's* The Martini *(Chronicle Books, 1956). Whichever recipe you prefer, remember that a Martini must be stirred and never shaken.*

Gin

Ingredients:

ice cubes
2½ measures gin
I measure dry vermouth
I lemon twist or I green olive

Variations:

This is just one recipe – there are many others, and all vary in the proportion of vermouth used. Why not find the proportion you enjoy the most and make your Martini your very own!

(For a 'vodka variation', see kangaroo in the vodka section, page 95).

Maiden's prayer

In the land of cocktails there are a number of maidens
– maiden's kiss, maiden's blush and even maiden-no-more.
Try this and maybe your prayers will be answered!

Ingredients:

ice cubes
2 measures gin
1 measure triple sec or
Cointreau
juice of 1 lemon
3 drops bitters

Variations:

Maiden-no-more?
Simply add a teaspoon of
brandy to the ingredients.

Gin

Method:

Half-fill the shaker with ice
cubes.
Add the bitters, lemon juice,
triple sec or Cointreau and
gin.
Shake well.
Strain and serve in a well-
chilled cocktail glass.
Close your eyes and pray!

method:	SHAKER
glass:	SOUR
garnish:	ORANGE SLICE AND A CHERRY

Orange blossom

This drink was born during Prohibition and is sometimes known as an Adirondack. Originally served straight up, it was simply a good slug of gin – probably bathtub gin – with a blush of orange juice to smooth it out. President Roosevelt shook one for Prime Minister Winston Churchill during World War Two. It seems that just one orange blossom was enough for the PM.

Gin

Method:

Half-fill the shaker with ice cubes.

Add the sugar, gin and orange juice.

Shake and then strain into a sour glass with plenty of ice or straight up if preferred.

Garnish with orange slice and cherry.

Ingredients:

ice cubes

1½ measures gin

1½ measures orange juice

½ teaspoon castor sugar

1 slice orange

1 cherry

Pink pussycat

*Grenadine is the ingredient that makes many cocktails pink:
pink elephant, pink squirrel and the pink panther.
The pink pussycat uses grapefruit juice – a juice that for some
unknown reason has been used to
torture the tastebuds into
waking up at the breakfast
table. Try this, and grapefruits
will take on a whole new meaning.*

Ingredients:

ice cubes
2 measures gin
2 measures grapefruit juice
2–3 measures pineapple juice
(depending on how sharp you
want your pussycat's claws!)
⅓ measure grenadine

Gin

Method:

Half-fill the shaker with ice
cubes.
Add the gin, pineapple and
grapefruit juices and the
grenadine.
Shake well and strain into an
ice-filled Collins glass.
Garnish with a slice of grapefruit (be brave!) and a cherry.

method:	MIXING GLASS
glass:	COCKTAIL
garnish:	TWIST OF LEMON

Silver bullet

*Many cocktails that have the word silver in their names
include raw egg white. A silver bullet, however, is eggless and
is a variation of the Martini. Like the Martini, you can vary the
proportion of Scotch to your taste.*

Ingredients:

ice cubes

2½ measures gin

1½ teaspoons Scotch whisky

1 lemon twist

Gin

Method:

Half-fill the mixing glass with
ice cubes.

Add the gin and Scotch and
stir well.

Strain into a chilled cocktail
glass and add the twist of
lemon.

White lady

This fabulous cocktail was invented by legendary bartender Harry MacElhone in 1919 while at Ciro's Club in London. In 1923, at his own Harry's New York Bar in Paris, MacElhone altered the recipe by replacing the original white crème de menthe with gin to create an internationally popular cocktail.

Gin

Ingredients:

ice cubes
1½ measures gin
1½ measures Cointreau
1½ measures lemon juice

Method:

Half-fill the shaker with ice cubes.
Pour in the lemon juice, Cointreau and gin and shake well.
Strain into a very cold cocktail glass.
Alternatively, you could serve it on the rocks in an old-fashioned glass.

Rum cocktails

El presidente
see page 64.

Rum is traditionally the drink of swash-buckling pirates and, you may be surprised to know, the first national spirit of Australia. Rum is, in effect, the glorious by-product of the manufacture of sugar. It was Christopher Columbus who introduced sugar cane to the Americas, and rum can be made from the fermented juices of the entire sugar cane, a speciality of South America called *aguardiente de caña* (literally 'fire-water from cane'). More familiar is the rum made from molasses, the heavy dark syrup left over after the solid sugar has been crystallised out of the sugar cane.

Raw sugar cane is pressed between rollers to extract the juice, which is then boiled down, clarified and put into machines which spin at high speeds and crystallise the sugar and separate it from the molasses. The molasses is reboiled to make a low-grade sugar and the residue is mixed with water and yeast, allowed to ferment and then distilled to produce rum.

Rums are divided into categories: light, medium, full bodied and aromatic. By law, each bottle must state its country of origin. You will also see rum that is called *añejo*: this means 'aged' rum. It generally has a tawny colour and more mellow flavour.

Light rum refers to its body, rather than its colour. A light rum may be colourless (so-called 'white rum') or it may be aged for three years to give more flavour and then be coloured with caramel. This is known as golden rum. Light rums are the style of the Spanish-speaking Caribbean, especially of Cuba, Puerto Rico and the Virgin Islands. Aged for more than six years, Puerto Rican rum may be called vieux or liqueur rum.

Medium-bodied rums are the speciality of the French speaking islands such as Martinique and Haiti, and are distilled from the juice of sugar cane rather than molasses. The juice is concentrated and distilled in pot stills and the rum is aged in oak casks, from which it takes it colour. From Guyana in Central America comes Demerara rum, made from the sugar produced in the area around the Demerara River. Although a very dark colour, it, too, has a medium body, often with a high alcohol content – 151 per cent proof – although strangely, it doesn't taste strongly alcoholic and can lull you into a false sense of security. Demerara rum is particularly good in hot toddies and grog and was sprinkled on the top of Don Beach's original zombie (see page 79).

Full-bodied rums come from Jamaica, where they are naturally fermented (with yeast from the air rather than cultured yeast, which settles on the surface of the 'mash') for about three weeks. It is then double-distilled: once to make a residue called dunder, and again to produce the more pungent rum. (An old insult is to call someone a 'dunderhead' – someone who is 'slow-witted' or whose mind has been dulled by excess rum.) It is then allowed to age in oak casks for no fewer than five years. Its colour is enhanced by the addition of caramel.

The final category of rum, aromatic, is used a great deal in The Netherlands and in Scandinavia. This is Batavia Arak, and comes from the island of Java, Indonesia (formerly the Dutch East Indies). Batavia refers to the town where this very dry and very pungent rum is made. The Arak is made from Javanese molasses into which small cakes of Javanese red rice are placed. This ferments naturally and the distilled rum is then shipped to Europe where it is aged for a further six years before it is blended and bottled.

Cuba libre
see page 60.

method:	BUILD
glass:	HIGHBALL
garnish:	HALF LEMON SHELL

Ingredients:

ice cubes

2 measures white rum
(preferably Bacardi)

½ measures triple sec
or Cointreau

juice of ½ lemon

4 measures ginger ale

spent shell of ½ lemon
to garnish

Rum

Method:

Add the lemon juice to a
highball glass two-thirds filled
with ice.

Drop in the spent shell of the
lemon and add the rum, triple
sec or Cointreau and top
with ginger ale.

Bacardi buck

*Bucks are tall drinks that are made by 'building' (directly adding
all the ingredients to an ice-filled glass). They have been around
since the late 19th century and consist of a base spirit, ginger ale
and lemon or lime juice. The traditional method is to squeeze half
a lemon or lime directly into the glass and then to drop in the spent
half shell. As usual, with all rules, there is an exception: bucks
made with white rum, such as the Bacardi buck, have a small
amount of another ingredient, such as a fruit juice or a
liqueur. This is also one of several drinks that uses the famous
brand of
Bacardi rum.*

Bacardi cocktail

The firm of Bacardi y Cia, proprietors of the Bacardi trademark, objected to the use (or misuse) of the name 'Bacardi' as applied to any drink not made with Bacardi rum. A New York Supreme Court Ruling in 1937 decreed in the firm's favour and Bacardi y Cie have exclusive rights to the use of the name.

Ingredients:

ice cubes
1½ measures Bacardi white rum
1 measure lime juice
(or lemon if preferred)
½ measure gomme syrup
1 teaspoon grenadine

Rum

Method:

Half-fill the shaker with ice cubes.
Add the lime (or lemon juice), grenadine, gomme syrup and Bacardi rum.
Shake well and strain into a champagne saucer/cocktail glass and garnish with a cherry on a stick.

Variations:

For a Bacardi flyer, make a Bacardi cocktail, strain into a large champagne saucer and top with chilled champagne.

For a Bacardi special, use 2 measures Bacardi rum, ¾ measure gin, 1 measure lime juice, 1 teaspoon grenadine and ½ teaspoon castor sugar. Shake all the ingredients except the rum until cold. Add the rum and shake again. Strain into a cocktail glass.

method:	BLENDER
glass:	GOBLET OR LARGE WINE GLASS

Batidas

A batida is a fruity Brazilian drink traditionally made with aguardiente de caña. This is the name given to the rums of South America, which are distilled from fermented and concentrated sugar-cane sap. The best known is Cachaca (pronounced cachasa) and is similar to unmatured white rum – full-bodied and a little 'raw'. Cachaca is available if you want to make a truly authentic batida, or you can use white rum in its place for a slightly 'smoother' taste.

Ingredients:

1 glass crushed ice
2 measures Cachaca
(or white rum)
4 oz fresh pineapple
cut into chunks
½ teaspoon granulated sugar

Rum

Method:

Place the crushed ice in the blender and add the Cachaca or white rum, pineapple chunks and sugar.
Blend until smooth and then pour into the goblet or wine glass.
Serve with short straws.

Batida abaci
(Pineapple batida)

Caipirinha

Pronounced 'cai-pir-een-i', it means '
'peasant's drink' in Brazil.
This lime-flavoured rum drink traditionally uses the
South American rum aguardiente de caña,
the best known of which is Cachaca
(see also the batidas).

Ingredients:

ice cubes
2½ measures Cachaca
(or white rum)
1 fresh lime
1½ teaspoons granulated sugar

Rum

Method:

Wash the lime and cut the
'knobs' from the top and tail.
Cut the lime into eight wedges.
Put the sugar in the glass, add
the lime wedges and crush
them until the juice is released
and the sugar dissolved.
Add the Cachaca or white rum
and muddle further to ensure
all the sugar is fully dissolved.
Add the ice cubes to the glass
and muddle some more.
Decorate with a slice of lime if
desired.

method:	BUILD
glass:	HIGHBALL
garnish:	SPENT SHELL OF $^{1}/_{2}$ LIME

Cuba libre

According to legend, an army officer in Havana, Cuba, invented this drink when he mixed Bacardi white rum with the newly arrived soft drink Coca Cola. If you ask a barman for a 'Bacardi and coke' you will be served exactly with these two registered brands. Ask for a Cuba libre and he will ask you which light rum you'd prefer!

Ingredients:

ice cubes
2 measures white rum
juice of $^{1}/_{2}$ lime
4–5 measures cold cola
spent shell of the lime
for garnish

Rum

Method:

Into a highball glass squeeze
the juice of $^{1}/_{2}$ lime.
Drop the spent shell of the
lime into the glass and then
fill the glass two-thirds full
with ice cubes.
Add the rum and top with
cold cola.
Serve with straws.

Variations:
Cuba libre supreme:

replace the rum with Southern
Comfort.

Cuba libre Espana:

$^{1}/_{2}$ measure of white rum,
$^{1}/_{2}$ measure dark rum, 1 measure
sweet sherry, juice 1/2 lime, cold
cola. Build into a highball glass as
for a Cuba libre.

Costa del Sol

Rum blends extremely well with other spirits. If you like a herbal lemony flavour, try this long, refreshing drink. Decorate it with a paper parasol and it will bring back memories of your holidays.

Viva Espana!

Ingredients:

ice cubes
2 measures white rum
1 measure rosso vermouth
1 measure gomme syrup
½ measure lemon juice
2–3 measures soda water
1 orange slice
1 maraschino cherry

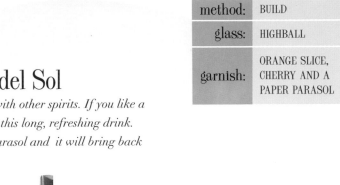

Rum

Method:

Fill the highball glass two-thirds full with ice cubes. Add the lemon juice, gomme syrup, rosso vermouth and rum.
Garnish with a slice of orange and a cherry. Decorate with the paper parasol. If it tastes too sweet, cut down on the gomme syrup or increase the lemon juice.

method:	SHAKER
glass:	COCKTAIL
garnish:	SLICE OF LIME

Daiquiri

The original Daiquiri, consisting of rum, lime and sugar, was created in Cuba in 1896 by an American mining engineer called Jennings Cox, who named the drink after the town of Daiquiri. Some say he ran out of gin and had to 'make do' with rum. Others say the rum was the only available 'medicine' to ward off malaria and the other ingredients were added by American workers to make it more palatable. The 'frozen' version of the classic Daiquiri cocktail was made famous in 1912 by Constantino 'Constante' Ribalagua at La Florida restaurant in Havana, Cuba.

Original
Daiquiri.

Rum

Method:

Half-fill the shaker with ice cubes.
Add the lime juice, castor sugar and rum.
Shake well and strain into a well-chilled cocktail glass.
Garnish with a lime slice.

Ingredients:

ice cubes
2 measures white rum
⅔ measure lime juice
1 teaspoon castor sugar
1 slice lime

Variations:

For a frozen Daquiri, add crushed ice to give it the consistency of a sherbet or sorbet. Shake and strain the ingredients into a glass filled with crushed ice

Diabolo

There is another devilish drink called a 'diablo' made with dry white port (see page 193). There is nothing hellish about either drink, however!

Ingredients:

crushed ice
2 measures rum
(of your choice)
½ measure triple sec
or Cointreau
½ measure dry vermouth
2 drops bitters
orange twist

Rum

Method:

Put some crushed ice in the shaker and pour on the vermouth, triple sec or Cointreau and rum. Add the bitters and shake. Strain and pour into a cocktail glass with a little crushed ice and garnish with the orange twist.

method:	SHAKER
glass:	OLD FASHIONED
garnish:	SLICE OF ORANGE AND A CHERRY

El Presidente

There are probably as many variations of the Presidente cocktail as there have been Latin American presidents. Some can be traced to an actual president, others go by the more general name of 'El Presidente'. The recipe offered here is for the Presidente created in around 1920 at the Vista Alegre Bar in Havana, Cuba, for President General Mario Menocal.

Ingredients:

ice cubes

crushed ice

2 measures white rum

1 measure rosso vermouth

⅓ measure dry vermouth

1 teaspoon grenadine

1 slice orange

1 cherry

Rum

Method:

Half-fill the shaker with ice cubes.

Add the grenadine, dry vermouth, rosso vermouth and white rum.

Shake well and strain into an old-fashioned glass almost filled with crushed ice, or, as the original version, straight up.

Garnish with the orange slice and cherry.

Grenada

This orange-and-cinnamon-flavored drink is named after Grenada, one of the Windward Islands in the West Indies.

Ingredients:

ice cubes

3 measures dark rum

1 measure rosso vermouth

1½ measures orange juice

ground cinnamon

Rum

Method:

Put some ice cubes in the mixing glass and add the orange juice, vermouth, and dark rum.

Stir well and strain into a chilled cocktail glass.

Sprinkle a little ground cinnamon on the top.

method:	BLENDER
glass:	GOBLET
garnish:	SLICE OF LIME

Havana Beach

A great party drink, it's also easy to make in large quantities using a blender or food processor. The lime is chopped up and distributed through the drink to form tiny green specks.

Rum

Method:

Cut the half-lime into four pieces and put them in the blender or food processor with the pineapple juice, sugar and rum.
Blend until smooth.
Put 3–4 ice cubes in a large goblet and pour in the mixture.
Top up with ginger ale and decorate with the lime slice.
Serve with straws.

Ingredients:

ice cubes
1 measure white rum
2 measures pineapple juice
½ lime
1 teaspoon sugar
4 measures ginger ale
1 lime slice

Jamaica Sunday

The full-bodied and aromatic rums of Jamaica are aged in oak vats for a minimum of five years. Some are still shipped to England for ageing and blending in bonded warehouses at ports in London and Liverpool and are known as London or Liverpool 'dock rums'. This recipe has an interesting ingredient – honey.

Ingredients:

broken ice
2 measures dark rum –
preferably Jamaican
1 teaspoon clear honey
½ measure lime juice
2 measures lemonade

Rum

Method:

Dissolve the honey in the rum and then pour into an old-fashioned glass filled with broken ice.
Top with lemonade and relax!

Method:	MUDDLE AND SHAKER
Glass:	COCKTAIL
Garnish:	CHOPPED, FRESH MINT

Maison Charles

A perfect, mint-flavored cocktail for a hot, summer evening.

Ingredients:

crushed ice

2 measures white rum

¼ measure lime juice

¼ measure gomme syrup

fresh mint

castor sugar

Rum

Method:

Gently crush one or two sprigs of mint in a mixing glass and cover with the rum. Let it stand for 20 minutes. Using a sharp knife, cut a few leaves of mint very finely – avoid using the central stem of the leaf. Mix a small amount of the chopped mint into the castor sugar to "frost" the rim of the glass. Run the lime peel around the rim of the glass and dip it in the sugar-mint mix. Put a glass of crushed ice into the shaker. Pour the "infused" rum into the shaker, along with the lime juice and gomme syrup. Shake well and strain into the frosted cocktail glass. Sprinkle a tiny amount of chopped mint on the top as a final decoration.

Variations:

For a Madison Avenue, replace the gomme syrup with Cointreau and make in the same manner as the Maison Charles.

Mojito

This is basically a Collins (see page 33), but made with rum and sprigs of mint – sometimes called the Cuban mint julep. The drink became popular in Cuba with Americans visiting the island during the Prohibition years.

Ingredients:

ice cubes

broken ice

2½ measures white rum

⅔ measure gomme syrup

1 dash bitters

juice of half a lime

2 measures soda water

3–4 sprigs mint

Rum

Method:

Gently crush the mint in the bottom of the glass.

Put the spent shell of the lime in the glass and fill with broken ice.

Half-fill the shaker with ice cubes.

Add the rum, lime juice, bitters, and gomme syrup.

Shake well and strain into the glass.

Add the soda and gently muddle together.

Add straws.

method:	BUILD
glass:	COLLINS
garnish:	SLICE OF GRAPEFRUIT AND A CHERRY

Monkey wrench

A refreshing, long drink that makes grapefruit juice taste wonderful. The lemonade cuts the sharpness of the juice. The cherry also helps!

Ingredients:

ice cubes
1¾ measures white rum
3 measures grapefruit juice
3 measures lemonade
slice of grapefruit
1 maraschino cherry

Rum

Method:

Fill a Collins glass two-thirds full with ice cubes.
Pour on the rum and grapefruit juice and top with lemonade.
Garnish with the grapefruit slice and cherry and add straws.

Northside special

This fruity drink was created at the Myrtle Bank Hotel
in Kingston, Jamaica, in the 1930s.

Ingredients:

broken ice
2 measures dark rum –
    preferably Jamaican
3 measures orange juice
½ measure lemon juice
2 teaspoons castor sugar
2 measures soda water
1 slice lemon
1 slice orange
1 cherry

Rum

Method:

In a Collins glass, dissolve the
sugar in the orange and
lemon juice.
Add the rum.
Fill the glass with broken ice
and top with soda.
Garnish with the orange and
lemon slices and the cherry.
Add straws.

Method:	SHAKER
Glass:	COCKTAIL
Garnish:	CHERRY ON A STICK

Petite Fleur

Both the name, meaning "little flower," and the addition of Cointreau suggest that this drink originated in the French-speaking islands of the Caribbean.

Ingredients:

ice cubes

1 measure white rum

1⅓ measures Cointreau

1⅓ measures grapefruit juice

1 maraschino cherry

Rum

Method:

Half-fill the shaker with ice cubes.

Pour in the grapefruit juice, Cointreau, and rum.

Shake well, strain into a cocktail glass, and add a cherry on a stick.

Pina Colada

One of the most popular drinks in the world, the pina colada was invented on the island of Puerto Rico and means "strained pineapple." Coconut cream is a vital ingredient of the pina colada: there are some pre-prepared brands available, but the best way is to make your own, since pure creamed coconut is easily obtained.

Ingredients:

crushed ice
2 measures light rum
5 measures pineapple juice (or 5 slices of tinned pineapple in its own juice, crushed in a blender)
1 measure coconut cream (made to recipe at left)
¼ slice pineapple
1 maraschino cherry

Rum

Method:

Pour the pineapple juice into the blender (or crush 5 slices of tinned pineapple in its own juice in a blender) and add the coconut cream and the rum.
Blend for a few seconds.
Add the crushed ice and blend for 5 seconds.
Pour into the goblet and garnish with the fruit.
Serve with a straw.

To Make Coconut Cream
Take a chilled, hard block of pure creamed coconut and grate it to break down the grainy texture. To make 1 pina colada, take 1 tablespoon of grated creamed coconut and 1 tablespoon of castor sugar and dissolve them in the smallest amount of hot water.
Stir until the texture is a smooth, runny paste. Taste to check on the sweetness and adjust as desired. Once cool, it's ready for use. Use the coconut cream the same day — don't store it as it will go off, taste absolutely disgusting, and turn into a grainy mess!

method:	BUILD
glass:	HIGHBALL
garnish:	LIME SLICE

Pink rum

A wonderful flavour and a gorgeous colour –
drink it while wearing a hibiscus
flower behind your ear!

Ingredients:

ice cubes
2 measures white rum
2 measures cranberry juice
1 measure soda water
3 drops bitters
1 slice lime

Rum

Method:

Put three drops of bitters
into a highball glass and swirl
them around so they coat
the inside of the glass.
Add some ice cubes and
pour in the rum and
cranberry juice.
Top with soda water and
decorate with the lime slice.

method:	SHAKER
glass:	HIGHBALL
garnish:	SLICE OF ORANGE, A CHERRY, PINEAPPLE WEDGE AND LIME WEDGE

75

Planter's punch

This famous drink was created to celebrate Fred L Myers'
founding of the Myer's Rum Distillery in Jamaica in 1879. There
are now several variations of the original recipe.

Ingredients:

ice cubes

1 measure dark rum
(preferably Myer's!)

1 measure light rum

1 measure añejo rum

1 measure orange juice

1 measure pineapple juice

½ measure grapefruit juice

1 teaspoon lime juice

1 teaspoon lemon juice

1 teaspoon grenadine

1 slice orange

1 pineapple wedge

1 lime wedge

1 maraschino sherry

Rum

Method:

Half-fill the shaker with ice
cubes.

Pour in the rums, lime and
lemon juice, orange juice,
pineapple and grapefruit
juices and the grenadine.
Shake well and strain into an
ice-filled highball glass and
garnish with the fruit.

Method:	MIXING GLASS
Glass:	OLD FASHIONED
Garnish:	SPENT SHELL OF ¼ LIME

Rum Ramsay

This drink was created around 1930 by barman Albert Martin at the Bon Ton Bar in New Orleans. The recipe was a secret for many years until he passed it on to Victor "Trader Vic" Bergeron. Martin originally served his Ramsay "straight up," but it was later popular served with broken ice.

Ingredients:

ice cubes
broken ice
1½ measures white rum
1 teaspoon bourbon
juice of ¼ lime
⅓ measure gomme syrup
1 dash bitters

Rum

Method:

Put some ice cubes in the mixing glass and squeeze the lime juice into it.
Drop in the spent shell. Add the rum, bourbon, and gomme syrup and stir well. Strain into an old-fashioned glass filled with broken ice (or serve straight up if preferred).

Santiago

Ingredients:

ice cubes
broken ice
1½ measures white rum
½ measure triple sec or Cointreau
1 teaspoon grenadine
½ measure gomme syrup
1 maraschino cherry

Rum

Method:

Half-fill the shaker with ice cubes. Pour in the rum, triple sec or Cointreau, grenadine, and gomme syrup.
Shake well and strain into an old-fashioned glass filled with broken ice.
Garnish with a maraschino cherry on a stick.

method:	SHAKER
glass:	HIGHBALL
garnish:	HALF A SPENT LIME SHELL

Scorpion

Definitely a drink with a sting in its tail!

Ingredients:

crushed ice

1 measure dark rum

¾ measure white rum

¾ measure brandy

¼ measure triple sec or
Cointreau

1½ measures orange juice

juice ½ lime

Rum

Method:

Put a glass of crushed ice in a
shaker.

Pour in the orange and lime
juice, white and dark rum,
brandy, triple sec or
Cointreau.

Shake well and strain into a
highball glass half-filled with
crushed ice.

Drop in the spent shell of the
lime.

Zombie prince

The original zombie was created in 1934 by legendary bartender Don Beach at the 'Don the Beachcomber' restaurant in Hollywood. It was made especially for a guest suffering from a hangover who reportedly said he felt 'like a zombie'. The object seems to have been to get as many different rums as possible into one drink: white rum, golden rum, dark rum and overproof dark rum, as well as cherry brandy and apricot brandy. The original zombie recipe has undergone various permutations from bar to bar. If you like rum, you'll love this 'regal' variation.

Ingredients:

crushed ice

1 measure white rum

1 measure golden rum

1 measure dark rum

3 drops bitters

1 teaspoon soft brown sugar

juice of 1 lemon

juice of 1 orange

juice of ½ grapefruit

lime slices

orange slices

Rum

Method:

Put just under a highball glassful of crushed ice into the mixing glass.

Pour on the lemon, orange and grapefruit juices.

Add the bitters and the sugar.

Pour in the three rums and stir vigorously.

Pour unstrained into a highball glass and garnish with the lime and orange slices.

Vodka Cocktails

Golden Russian
see page 91.

Vodka is a paradox among spirits, for it has no taste, no aroma, and no color. It is nothing more (and nothing less) than pure, high-proof grain alcohol (usually wheat, corn, or rye, with a little added malt), and water. Nevertheless, vodka can, in fact, be made from any manner of ingredients: in the Czech Republic, potatoes are used; in Turkey, they use beets, in Britain, molasses, while in the United States, vodka is made from grains. It is the starch in these ingredients that produces the ethyl alcohol in the distillation process.

The word "vodka" is a diminutive of the Russian *voda*, meaning "water"; vodka is literally "little water," but this "little water" can pack a very strong punch! Vodkas are available from 35 to the 80 percent proof of pure Polish spirit. Vodka was mentioned as early as the 12th century in Russian literature, but at the time it referred to any spirit, regardless of how it was distilled or flavored. By the 17th century, vodka played an important part in both civil and religious ceremonies. It was served at all imperial banquets and was drunk ceremonially at religious festivals and as part of church ritual.

Poland and Russia continue to produce a wide variety of spiced and fruit versions and in a range of colors. The most celebrated is the delicately flavored "Zubrowka," with a blade of grass in each bottle – which also gives it a yellow-green color. The grass is that

that found most appetising to the wild European bison which graze on the borders of Poland and Russia. Pertsovka and Okhotchinaya are fiery 'pepper' vodkas, the former infused with cayenne and capsicum, the latter with additional herbs, and are said to have been 'invented' by Tsar Peter the Great, who added pepper to his drink. One governor of Moscow apparently trained a large bear to serve pepper vodka to his guests. If they declined, the bear removed the unfortunate guest's clothes one item at a time. You can make your own pepper vodka by steeping a hot Mexican or Italian pepper in a bottle of neutral vodka and leaving it there for as long as possible.

Jarzebiak is flavoured with rowan berries (the fruit of the mountain ash) and is a delicate pink colour. Lemon vodka, with a yellow colour, can also be easily made at home by grating a small quantity of lemon peel, letting it dry for two or three days and then adding it to the bottle. Allow it to stand for around ten days, shaking it occasionally, and then decant the liquid.

The aim of producing unflavoured vodka was not simply for the neutral spirit to make a wonderful base for mixed drinks. The original purpose was, in fact, to produce a strong spirit that would not freeze in the extreme cold of the Eastern European winters! Filtering the spirit through charcoal or fine quartz sand removes the aroma and taste. Vodka is not aged, but bottled straightaway. There is, however, a spirit called Starka (which means 'old') vodka, which has been aged in wine casks for ten years.

Harvey Wallbanger
see page 92.

method:	BUILD (OR CAN BE SHAKEN)
glass:	HIGHBALL
garnish:	CELERY STICK WITH LEAVES (OPTIONAL), WEDGE OF LIME

Bloody Mary

Harry's New York Bar in Paris in 1921 was the birthplace of this classic drink. In 1921 barman Fernand 'Pete' Petiot mixed tomato juice, vodka, salt, pepper and Worcestershire sauce. While there was nothing new about the combination of vodka and tomato, the name was. According to many accounts, Petiot named his mix in honour of Hollywood actress Mary Pickford.

The celery-stick garnish originated in the 1960s: when a drinker at the Pump Room in the Ambassador Hotel in Chicago received his Bloody Mary without the usual swizzle stick, he picked up a celery stick from a tray of crudites and used it to stir his drink and the garnish was born. Eat your garnish if you want to!

Vodka

Method:

In a highball glass two-thirds filled with ice cubes, pour the tomato juice, lemon (or lemon and lime) juice and the vodka.

Add the spices and stir.

Garnish with the lime wedge and celery stick.

Add a stirrer.

Play around with the quantities of spices and sauces: some people like it 'mild', some, as they say, like it 'hot'!

Ingredients:

ice cubes

2 measures vodka

5 measures tomato juice

½ teaspoon lemon juice
(or a less sharp mix using lemon and lime juice if preferred)

2–3 dashes Worcestershire sauce

1–2 dashes Tabasco sauce
(or more if you like it spicy)

1 pinch salt
(celery salt if possible)

1 pinch black pepper

1 celery stalk with leaves
(optional)

Brazen hussy

The name conjures up images of 'jazz babies' and platinum-blonde Hollywood starlets.

Ingredients:

ice cubes
1 measure vodka
1 measure triple sec or
Cointreau
1½ measures lemon juice

Vodka

Method:

Hall-fill the shaker with ice cubes.
Add all the ingredients and shake well.
Strain into a cocktail glass.

method:	BUILD
glass:	HIGHBALL
garnish:	LEMON WEDGE

Bullfrog

A lovely, long drink for a hot summer's evening.

Ingredients:

ice cubes

2 measures vodka

1 teaspoon triple sec or
Cointreau

4 measures lemonade

1 lemon wedge

Vodka

Method:

Almost fill the highball glass
with ice cubes.

Add the vodka, triple sec or
Cointreau and lemonade.

Stir well and garnish with the
lemon wedge.

Cape Codder

If you like the dryness of cranberry juice, try this out. Simple and delicious, it's a refreshing alternative to the usual 'vodka-tonic' combination.

Ingredients:

ice cubes
2 measures vodka
5 measures cranberry juice
1 lime wedge

Vodka

Method:

Almost fill the highball glass with ice cubes.
Pour in the vodka and cranberry juice and stir well.
Garnish with the lime wedge.

method:	SHAKER
glass:	COCKTAIL
garnish:	TWIST OF LIME

Cosmopolitan

A relatively new drink from America, the cosmopolitan is a Martini-style aperitif that's growing in popularity.

Ingredients:

ice cubes
1½ measures vodka
1 measure triple sec
or Cointreau
1 dash cranberry juice
(or to taste)
1 lime twist

Vodka

Method:

Half-fill the shaker with ice cubes.
Add the vodka, triple sec or Cointreau and cranberry juice.
Shake sharply and strain into well-chilled cocktail glass.
Garnish with the lime twist and discard.

Variations:

Adjust the measures of cranberry juice to suit your taste. You could even add some more lime juice if you want your cosmopolitan a little more sour.

Cooch Behar

*This drink was devised by the Maharajah of Cooch Behar,
and it's a great drink to have with a curry.
Although an Indian recipe, the vodka used originally was a
Russian pepper vodka, such as Okhotnichaya.
You can make your own pepper vodka quite easily:
simply steep a hot Mexican or Italian pepper in regular
vodka for a few weeks.*

Ingredients:

ice cubes
2 measures pepper vodka
4 measures tomato juice

Vodka

Method:

Half-fill the shaker with ice
cubes.
Add the vodka and tomato
juice and shake thoroughly.
Strain and serve on the rocks
in an old-fashioned glass.

method:	SHAKER
glass:	COLLINS OR HIGHBALL

Down-under fizz

This attractive-looking drink pays homage to the Antipodes. The clear top of soda water floats on the vodka, grenadine and orange juice 'sun' at the bottom of the glass to be sucked up through a straw!

Ingredients:

ice cubes

3 measures vodka

½ measure lemon juice

1 measure orange juice

½ teaspoon grenadine

soda water

Vodka

Method:

Half-fill the shaker with ice cubes.

Add the lemon and orange juice, grenadine and vodka. Shake well and pour unstrained into a Collins/highball glass. Top with soda water and serve with a straw.

Fire and ice

Use some more of the pepper vodka you've made
(see page 87) in this neat little cocktail.

Ingredients:

ice cubes
2 measures pepper vodka
1½ teaspoons dry
vermouth

Vodka

Method:

Half-fill the mixing glass with
ice cubes.
Add the pepper vodka and
dry vermouth and stir well.
Strain into a cocktail glass.
As with the Martini, try
different proportions of the
vermouth until you find the
one you like best.

| method: | BUILD |
| glass: | HIGHBALL |

Ingredients:

ice cubes

2 measures vodka

4 measures grapefruit juice

1 teaspoon grenadine

Vodka

Method:

Almost fill a highball glass
with ice cubes.
Pour the vodka and
grapefruit juice into the glass.
Drop the grenadine carefully
into the centre of the drink.
If you really like the
sharpness of the juice, leave
out the grenadine and you'll
have made yourself a
greyhound.

Firefly

*Not only is this an attractive drink, it's
the best way to drink grapefruit juice!
The grenadine is just enough to cut
through the sour of the juice.*

Golden Russian

Many vodka-based drinks inevitably have names associated with Russia, such as the Soviet (page 103) and the Moscow mule (page 99). Try a golden Russian on a cold, snowy night!

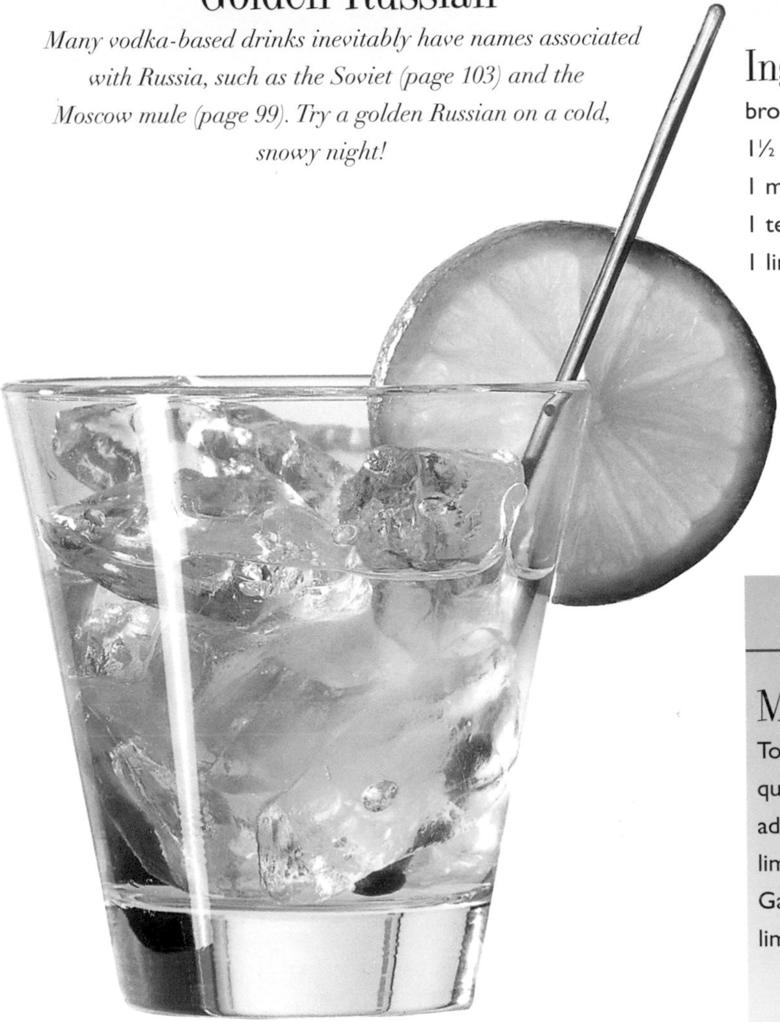

Ingredients:

broken ice
1½ measures vodka
1 measure Galliano
1 teaspoon lime juice
1 lime slice

Vodka

Method:

To a highball glass, three-quarters full of broken ice, add the vodka, Galliano and lime juice and mix gently. Garnish with the slice of lime.

Variations:

If you use the Italian liqueur Strega (a sweet and spicy mix made from more than 70 herbs, said to have been created by beautiful maidens who, for some unknown reason, disguised themselves as witches), you'll make a warlock.

method:	SHAKER
glass:	HIGHBALL
garnish:	ORANGE SLICE

Harvey Wallbanger

Harvey, according to the legend, was a California surfer. After losing an important contest, he consoled himself with a screwdriver, but added a dash of Galliano. After several drinks, he tried to leave the bar, but unfortunately kept bumping into furniture and the wall. Harvey 'the Wallbanger' became his nickname and the famous drink was born.

Ingredients:

ice cubes
2 measures vodka
¾ measure Galliano
5 measures orange
juice

Vodka

Method:

Half-fill the shaker with ice
cubes.
Add the vodka and orange
juice and shake well.
Strain into an ice-filled
highball glass.
Gently float the Galliano on
top and garnish with the
orange slice.

Hawaiian vodka

The tropical sunshine of Hawaii melts the icy heart of the
Russian steppes in this delicious and refreshing mix.

Ingredients:

ice cubes
3 measures vodka
I measure pineapple juice
I measure orange juice
I measure lemon juice
I teaspoon grenadine
I lemon slice

Vodka

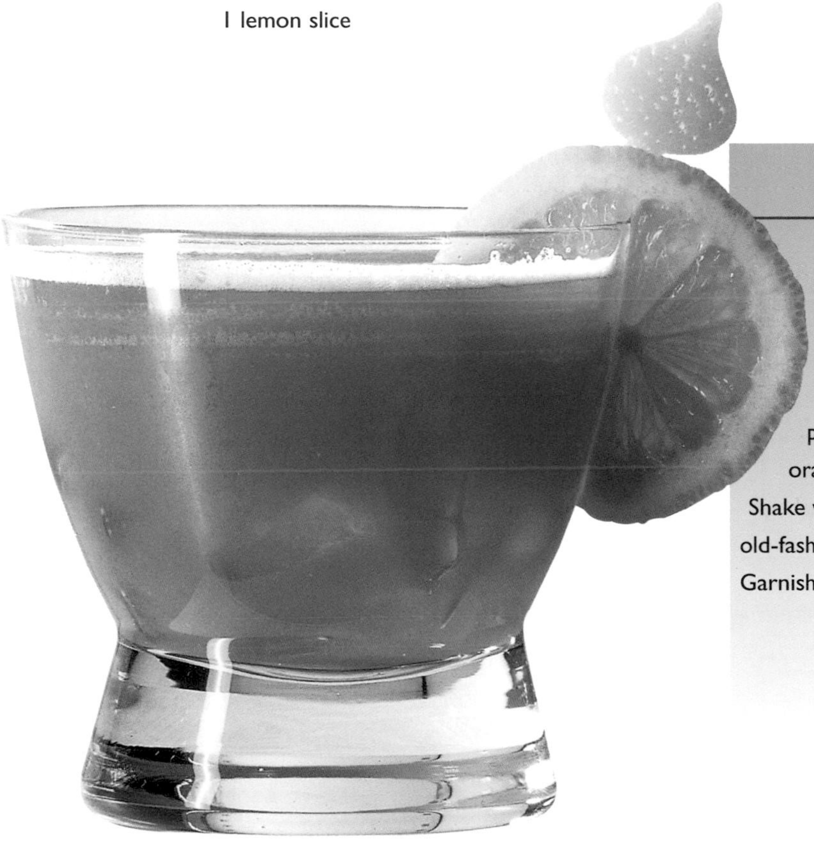

Method:

Half-fill the shaker
with ice cubes.
Pour in the
pineapple, lemon and
orange juice and vodka.
Shake well and strain into an
old-fashioned glass.
Garnish with the lemon slice.

method:	MIXING GLASS
glass:	COCKTAIL

Kamikaze

Kamikaze is the Japanese for 'divine wind'.
The original drink, made with Stolichnaya vodka and a teaspoon
of Rose's Lime Juice, was drunk in one go – as fast as the wind –
and was designed to get a person drunk quickly.

Ingredients:

ice cubes

2 measures vodka

1 teaspoon Rose's Lime Juice

Vodka

Method:

Half-fill the mixing glass with ice cubes.

Add the vodka and lime juice.

Stir well and strain into a cocktail glass.

Drink in one go.

method:	MIXING GLASS
glass:	COCKTAIL (OR ON THE ROCKS IN AN OLD-FASHIONED GLASS IF YOU PREFER)
garnish:	GREEN OLIVE OR A TWIST OF LEMON (AS PREFERRED)

Kangaroo

This is what some people might call a 'vodkatini'. The original Martini (page 48) was gin-based, but this vodka version is increasingly popular and, like the original, is stirred.

Ingredients:

ice cubes
2 measures vodka
1 measure dry vermouth
1 green olive or 1 lemon twist

Vodka

Method:

Half-fill the mixing glass with ice cubes.
Add the vodka and the dry vermouth and stir.
Strain into a chilled cocktail glass (or strain over ice cubes in an old-fashioned glass).
Garnish with the green olive or twist of lemon if preferred.

method:	MIXING GLASS
glass:	COCKTAIL
garnish:	LEMON TWIST

Laughing at the waves
You probably will be after one of these!

Ingredients:
ice cubes
1½ measures vodka
½ measures dry vermouth
½ measure Campari
1 lemon twist

Vodka

Method:
Half-fill the mixing glass with ice cubes.
Add the vodka, dry vermouth and Campari.
Stir well and strain into a cocktail glass.
Garnish with the lemon twist.

Long Island Iced Tea

This drink could actually be placed in several sections of
this book since it contains equal measures of vodka, gin, rum,
tequila, and triple sec. In early versions, however,
the tequila and triple sec were omitted.

Ingredients:

ice cubes
broken ice
½ measure vodka
½ measure gin
½ measure tequila
½ measure white rum
½ measure triple sec
or Cointreau
1 measure lemon juice
½ measure gomme
syrup
3–4 measures cold cola
1 lemon wedge

Variations:

Leave out the triple sec or
Cointreau for Texas tea. Use
lemonade instead of cola, and
you have Long Island
lemonade. For Long Beach
iced tea, use cranberry
juice in place of the
cola.

Vodka

Method:

Half-fill the shaker with
ice cubes.
Add the vodka, gin, rum,
tequila, triple sec or
Cointreau, lemon juice, and
gomme syrup.
Shake well and strain into a
Collins glass half-full of
broken ice.
Add the cola and garnish
with the lemon wedge.

method:	BUILD
glass:	HIGHBALL

Madras

*The colour of this drink is similar to the famous bright
cottons and silks of Madras in southern India.*

Ingredients:

ice cubes
1½ measures vodka
2 measures cranberry juice
2 measures orange juice

Vodka

Method:

Fill a highball glass two-thirds
full with ice cubes.
Pour in the orange juice,
cranberry juice and vodka
and stir.

method:	BUILD
glass:	COLLINS OR HIGHBALL
garnish:	ORANGE AND LIME SLICES

Moscow mule

Despite its name, the Moscow mule is an American invention. In 1947, John Martin, of Heublin & Co, USA, who had acquired the rights to Smirnoff vodka, was trying to find ways to encourage sales. A chance conversation with Jack Morgan, of the Cock 'n' Bull Saloon in Los Angeles, revealed that Morgan was overstocked with ginger ale. They added the two, with a dash of lime juice, and created the Moscow mule, which they originally served in a copper mug. Adjust the amount of vodka to vary the mule's kick.

Ingredients:

broken ice cubes
2 measures vodka
1 measure lime juice
4 measures ginger ale
1 lemon and 1 orange slice

Variations:

Try a Moscow mule with ginger beer in place of ginger ale.

Vodka

Method:

Almost fill the highball (or Collins) glass with broken ice.
Pour in the vodka and lime juice.
Add the ginger ale and stir well.
Garnish with the lemon and orange slices, or, for a change, try a slice of cucumber.

Method:	SHAKER
Glass:	HIGHBALL

Purple Passion

The purple comes from the addition
of red grape juice.

Ingredients:

ice cubes

2 measures vodka

2 measures grape juice

2 measures grapefruit juice

1–2 teaspoons castor sugar

(according to taste)

Vodka

Method:

Half-fill the shaker with ice cubes.

Add the grape juice and the grapefruit juice.

Add the sugar and then the vodka.

Shake well and strain into a highball glass two-thirds full of ice cubes.

Salty Dog

This is basically a drink known as a greyhound,
but the difference is that the rim of the highball glass is
"frosted" with salt. Try it and see.

Ingredients:

ice cubes
2 teaspoons salt
2 measures vodka
5 measures grapefruit juice
1 lime wedge

Vodka

Method:

Place the salt in a saucer.
Rub the rim of the highball
glass with the wedge of lime.
Dip the glass into the salt to
coat the rim thoroughly.
Discard the lime.
Fill the glass two-thirds full
with ice cubes.
Half-fill the shaker with ice
cubes.
Add the vodka and grapefruit
juice and shake well.
Strain into the glass.

Variations:

For added decoration, why not add a spiral of grapefruit peel? Cut a
thin (as thin as possible) continuous spiral of peel and drape it over
the rim of the glass. Spirals can be cut from any citrus fruit and are the
"traditional" garnish of drinks called "coolers" (see page 162).

method:	BUILD
glass:	HIGHBALL
garnish:	LIME WEDGE

Ingredients:

ice cubes

1½ measures vodka

2 measures grapefruit juice

3 measures cranberry juice

1 lime wedge

Sea breeze

This drink has undergone some changes since it was first invented. In the 1930s, it was made with gin and grenadine. The more modern version uses vodka, cranberry and grapefruit juice to create a long, fruity drink.

Vodka

Method:

Almost fill the highball glass with ice cubes.

Add the vodka, cranberry and grapefruit juices.

Stir well.

Garnish with the lime wedge.

Variations:

Still not happy with grapefruit juice? Try pineapple juice instead for a bay breeze!

Soviet

A toast to Glasnost! One for the James Bonds of the new millennium, perhaps?

Ingredients:

ice cubes

3 measures vodka

½ measure dry vermouth

½ measure dry sherry

Vodka

Method:

Place the ice cubes in the old-fashioned glass.
Add the vodka, vermouth and sherry and stir. *Prosit!*

Method:	SHAKER
Glass:	COLLINS/ HIGHBALL
Garnish:	CHERRY

Slow, Comfortable Screw
Against the Wall

One of those incredibly named drinks that everyone's heard about. It's "slow" because it should properly use sloe gin (basically gin which has had sloe berries macerated in it); "comfortable" because it uses Southern Comfort (a well-known proprietary blend of bourbon and peach liqueur); "screw" from the screwdriver, but with the Galliano of the Harvey Wallbanger, hence "against the wall." You may wish to try one!

Ingredients:

ice cubes
broken ice
1 measure vodka
¾ measure Southern Comfort
¾ measure gin – preferably
sloe gin
½ measure Galliano
5 measures orange juice
1 cherry

Vodka

Method:

Half-fill the shaker with ice cubes.

Add the vodka, Southern Comfort, gin, and orange juice.

Shake and strain into the highball or Collins glass filled with broken ice.

Float the Galliano on the top and garnish with the cherry.

Add straws and a muddler (or use a screwdriver if you prefer).

Volga

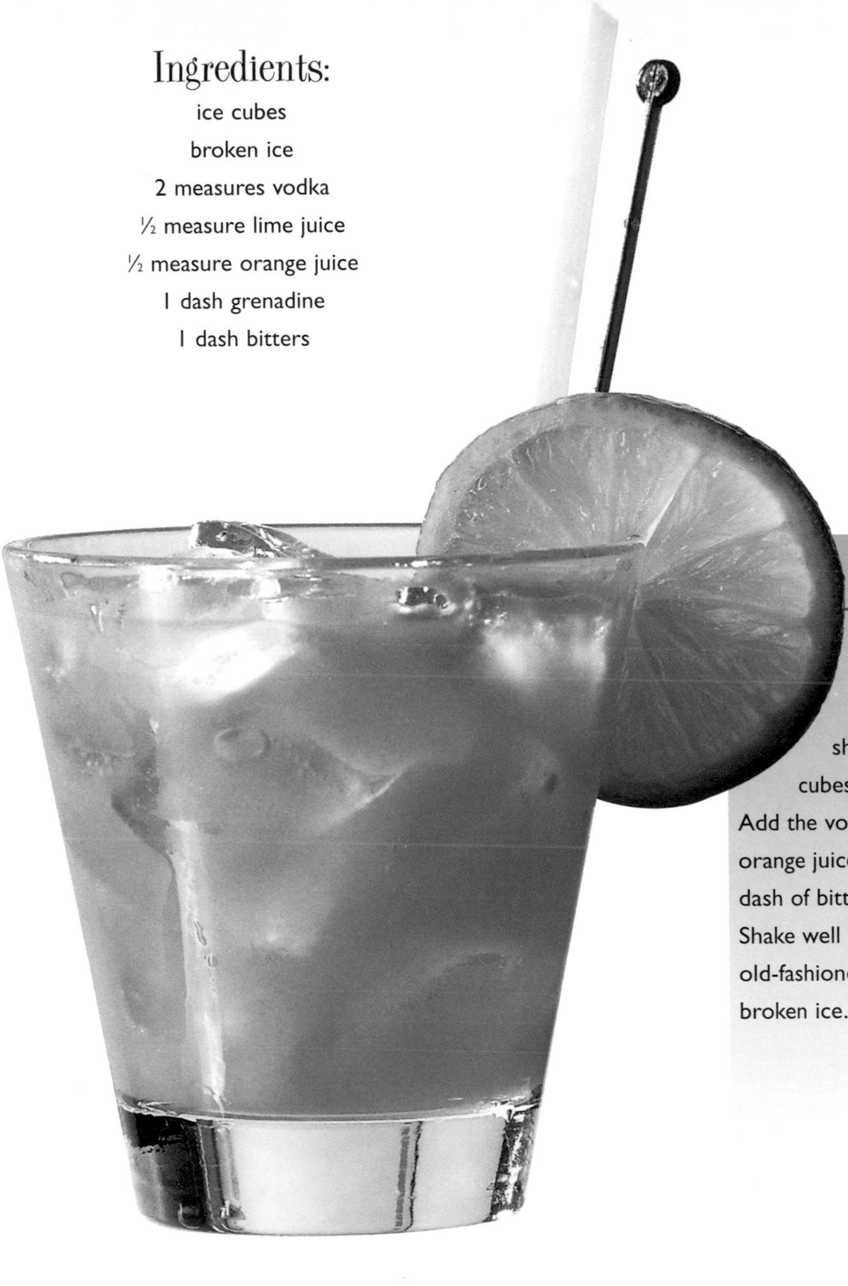

Ingredients:

ice cubes
broken ice
2 measures vodka
½ measure lime juice
½ measure orange juice
1 dash grenadine
1 dash bitters

Vodka

Method:

Half-fill the shaker with ice cubes.

Add the vodka, lime and orange juice, grenadine, and dash of bitters.

Shake well and strain into an old-fashioned glass filled with broken ice.

Whisky cocktails

The word whisky is a corruption of the Gaelic *usige beatha*, or *uisgebaugh*, which mean ' water of life'. There is whisky and there is whiskey: in Scotland and Canada, there is no 'e', while in America and Ireland, it's whiskey. Each of the whisk(e)y-producing countries has its own style and there are many different varieties of whiskies.

Scotch is whisky from Scotland and nowhere else. It cannot be made in England or America, although it can be imported for blending and bottling in different countries. Most Scotch whiskies are blended, often from the products of several distilleries. At least 60 per cent of a blend will be made of grain whiskies, with the rest from malts (barley that has been germinated to release fermentable sugars and then heated to stop the germination process) in order to achieve the balance of taste that each brand is known for. An unblended malt whisky is commonly described as being a single malt. The individual flavours of Scotch whiskies are derived from several influencing factors: the water from which they are made; the peat over which the water flows; the air surrounding the cask during maturation; the shape of the pot still; and the oak casks in which the whisky is aged.

The Irish were probably the first people to make whiskey, and their secrets of distillation were exported with monks to Scotland in the early Middle Ages. Where the Scots use a peat fire to dry their barley (and which influences the flavour), the

Manhattan
see page 116.

Irish dry theirs in a kiln using coal. Furthermore, the Irish are unique in that they use uncooked cereal (usually unmalted barley) and triple distillation in pot stills (Scotch is twice-distilled).

The main ingredient of bourbon is corn. It was in Bourbon County, Kentucky, that America's first corn whiskey was made. Today, half the bourbon distilleries in the US are in Kentucky. Some say it was distiller John Ritchie who made it at Lin's Fort, near Bardstown, in 1777, others credit the Reverend Elijah Craig of Georgetown in 1789. Bourbon is made in a continuous still from a fermented cereal mash – by law bourbon must be a minimum of 51 per cent corn, but in practice it is more likely to be 60 to 80 per cent and matured in new, charred, white-oak barrels for a minimum of two years, but generally for between six and eight years. Under US laws, the casks can only be used a single time. Once used, the casks are sought after by the distillers of Caribbean rums for their produce. Sour mash is a style of bourbon: a proportion of the mash already used in a previous distillation (hence 'sour') is added to the fresh mash about to be used. One of the most famous sour-mash whiskies is Jack Daniel's from Lynchburg, Tennessee. A Tennessee whiskey must be made in that state and must be made from at least 51 per cent of any one grain.

Rye whiskey was probably the first whiskey ever to be produced in the United States, made by Irish and Scottish immigrants to the New World in the 17th century. Rye must be made with a minimum of 51 per cent of the grain that gives it its name, and, like bourbon, is distilled in a continuous still and aged in charred, new oak barrels for not less than one year.

The smooth-bodied whiskies manufactured in Canada are made from cereal grains such as barley, corn, wheat and rye (both malted and rye grain) in varying proportions according to individual makers. Both old and new casks are used for ageing, which must be for a minimum of three years, although six years is more common.

Rebel raider
see page 121.

Method:	MIXING GLASS
Glass:	COCKTAIL
Garnish:	TWIST OF LEMON

Affinity

A classic cocktail from Harry Craddock's The Savoy Cocktail Book, the affinity was one of the most fashionable aperitifs of the 1920s.

Ingredients:

ice cubes

1 measure Scotch whisky

1 measure rosso vermouth

1 measure dry vermouth

1 dash bitters

1 lemon twist

Whisky

Method:

Half-fill the mixing glass with ice cubes and pour in the two vermouths.

Add the Scotch and the dash of bitters and stir.

Strain into a cocktail glass and squeeze the lemon twist over the glass and then discard it.

Artist's Special

This fruity, Scotch-flavored cocktail was invented at the Artists' Club in the Rue Pigalle, Paris, in the 1920s. It was typically avant-garde of artists to disregard the sanctity and tradition associated with Scotch whisky.

Ingredients:

ice cubes
1 measure Scotch
1 measure sherry
½ measure grenadine
½ measure lemon juice

Whisky

Method:

Half-fill the shaker with ice cubes and pour in the lemon juice and grenadine.
Add the sherry and the Scotch and shake well.
Strain into a cocktail glass.

Algonquin

From the famous hotel of the same name, this drink makes use of rye, the first whiskey of the United States.

Ingredients:

ice cubes

broken ice

2 measures rye

1 measure dry vermouth

1 measure pineapple juice

Whisky

Method:

Half-fill the shaker with ice cubes.

Pour in the pineapple juice, vermouth and rye.

Shake and strain into an old-fashioned glass three-quarters filled with broken ice.

The bairn

In Scotland and the north-east of England,
a 'bairn' is a child. There is, however,
nothing juvenile about this drink.

Ingredients:

broken ice
2 measures Scotch
¾ measure Cointreau
1 teaspoon Campari

Whisky

Method:

Fill an old-fashioned glass
three-quarters full with
broken ice.
Pour in the Cointreau and
Scotch and add the Campari.
Serve with a stirrer.

Method:	SHAKER
Glass:	HIGHBALL
Garnish:	SLICE OF LEMON

Cablegram

Perhaps someone will devise an "e-mail cocktail"!
Traditionally, this drink uses Canadian whisky;
a blended whisky works just as well.

Ingredients:

ice cubes
1½ measures Canadian
whisky/blended whisky
½ measure lemon juice
½ teaspoon castor sugar
4 measures ginger ale
1 lemon slice

Whisky

Method:

Half-fill the shaker with ice
cubes.
Add the lemon juice, sugar,
and whisky and shake well.
Strain into a highball glass
almost filled with ice cubes
and garnish with the slice of
lemon.

Fancy Bourbon

It is said that a little of what you fancy does you good. In fact, you can make fancies with gin, Scotch, or brandy, as well as bourbon.

Ingredients:

ice cubes

broken ice

2 measures bourbon

½ teaspoon triple sec or
Cointreau

½ teaspoon castor sugar

2 dashes bitters

1 lemon twist

Whisky

Method:

Half-fill the shaker with ice cubes.

Pour in the triple sec or Cointreau and bourbon.

Add the sugar and the bitters and shake well. Strain into an old-fashioned glass three-quarters filled with broken ice.

Method:	SHAKER
Glass:	OLD-FASHIONED
Garnish:	LIME WEDGE

Golden Daisy

We've already met the daisy in the section on gin (page 41), but there is a growing consensus that bourbon makes one of the finest drinks. While the original daisies included a fruit syrup (such as grenadine), this golden daisy includes Cointreau. Try this version and see what you think.

Ingredients:

ice cubes

broken ice

½ measure bourbon

½ measure Cointreau

1 measure lemon juice

1 lime wedge

Whisky

Method:

Half-fill the shaker with ice cubes.

Pour in the lemon juice, Cointreau, and bourbon and shake vigorously.

Strain into an old-fashioned glass half-filled with broken ice and garnish with the lime wedge.

The Highball

So popular was this drink, that in the 1920s
The New York Times set out to discover the truth about its
origins. Investigations proved that some time around 1895,
New York barman Patrick Duffy created the highball, a drink
which took its name from the 19th-century American
railroad practice of raising a ball on a high pole as a signal
to train drivers to increase their speed. Since a "highball"
meant "hurry," Duffy devised a drink that could also be
made quickly by simply pouring the ingredients over ice in
a tall glass.

Ingredients:

ice cubes
½ measure bourbon
5 measures soda
(or ginger ale)

Whisky

Method:

Drop 3 or 4 ice cubes into
the highball glass.
Pour in the bourbon and top
with soda or ginger ale.
Add the lemon twist
(optional).
Stir lightly.

Variations:

Add 2 dashes of bitters,
and you've got horse
feathers.

Method:	SHAKER
Glass:	OLD-FASHIONED
Garnish:	MARASCHINO CHERRY

Manhattan

You've been to the Bronx (page 30), now visit Manhattan!
One of the basic, classic cocktails, the Manhattan is reputed to
have been invented in around 1874 at the Manhattan Club in New
York for Winston Churchill's mother, Lady Randolph Churchill.
Originally, a Manhattan was made with 1 measure whiskey and 2
measures vermouth and served straight up. Today, they are more
often served on the rocks and with a lot less vermouth. Rye
whiskey was used, but many prefer bourbon.

Ingredients:

ice cubes

broken ice

2 measures rye or bourbon

1 measure rosso vermouth

1 dash bitters

1 maraschino cherry

Whisky

Method:

Put a glassful of broken ice
into the shaker.
Pour in the whiskey and
vermouth and add a dash of
bitters.
Shake briefly and pour
unstrained into an old-
fashioned glass.
Add the cherry.

As with the Martini (page 48), experiment with the proportions
of whisky and vermouth to suit your taste.

Mint Julep

Traditionally served on Kentucky Derby Day – the first Saturday in May – no other
tall drink is so delicious – and no other is likely to cause as much debate as to how to make it.
Do you crush the mint or not? Do you leave it in the glass or take it out? Should you drink it
through a straw? An early record of the mint julep was written by an English teacher,
John Davis, in 1803, while he was working in Virginia. He
described the julep as a "dram of spirituous liquor that has
mint in it" and also noted that the Virginians drank
it in the mornings as an "eye-opener." The
"spirituous liquor" Davis mentioned was
most likely brandy. After the Civil
War, bourbon became more widely
available and this has continued
to be the most popular
base spirit for
mint juleps.

Whisky

Ingredients:

crushed ice – crushed as fine as
possible – the more like snow
the better!
3 measures bourbon –
Kentucky bourbon is best
1 measure gomme syrup
4 sprigs mint – use small,
tender leaves. Use more if you
like more mint!
mint sprigs for garnish

Method:

Pre-chill the Collins glass. Pour in
the gomme syrup and add the
sprigs of mint. Gently crush the
mint with a muddler. How much
juice you crush out of the mint
leaves is up to you. (Some flatly
refuse to crush them at all.) Add
the bourbon and stir gently while
filling the glass with crushed ice.
Clip off the end of each sprig of
mint so that the juice flows into
the julep and arrange the sprigs
of mint on top. Serve with
straws and a stirrer.

Method:	SHAKER
Glass:	OLD-FASHIONED
Garnish:	TWIST OF ORANGE

New York

A toast to the Big Apple!

Ingredients:

ice cubes

broken ice

2 measures whisky –
traditionally, Canadian whisky

¾ measure lime juice

½ measure gomme syrup

1 teaspoon grenadine

Whisky

Method:

Half-fill the shaker with ice cubes.

Pour in the lime juice, gomme syrup, grenadine, and whisky. Shake well and strain into an old-fashioned glass three-quarters filled with broken ice.

Add the twist of orange.

Variation:

Replace the Canadian whisky with bourbon, and leave out the gomme syrup, and you have a New Yorker.

Method:	BUILD
Glass:	OLD-FASHIONED
Garnish:	SLICE OF LEMON AND CHERRY (some prefer a slice or twist of orange)

119

Old-fashioned

This classic whiskey cocktail – made with American whiskey, but some will argue specifically for rye – first appeared at the Pendennis Club in Louisville, Kentucky, in 1900. It was made especially at the request of bourbon distiller Colonel James E. Pepper. It's simply bourbon added to a glass containing a bitters-soaked sugar cube and then filled with ice – but some advocate sugar muddled in a little water.

Ingredients:

broken ice
2 measures bourbon
1 sugar cube
1 dash bitters
1 dash soda water (optional)

Variations:

Old-fashioneds don't have to
be bourbon: replace the
whiskey with the base spirit
of your choice.

Whisky

Method:

Place the sugar cube in the old-fashioned glass. Add the dash of bitters. When the sugar cube has soaked up all of the bitters, three-quarters fill the glass with broken ice. Pour in the whiskey.
Add the garnish and dash of soda water (optional) and serve with a muddler.

Method:	SHAKER
Glass:	OLD-FASHIONED

Opening

A classic cocktail and a perfect, pretheater or interval drink.

Ingredients:

ice cubes

1 measure whisky

2 teaspoons rosso vermouth

2 teaspoons grenadine

Whisky

Method:

Half-fill the shaker with ice cubes.

Pour in the whisky, vermouth, and grenadine and shake vigorously.

Strain into an old-fashioned glass two-thirds filled with ice cubes.

Rebel Raider

A number of mixed drinks have "rebel" in their names: rebel rouser, rebel yell, and this, the rebel raider. Rebs (short for rebels) was the name given to Confederate soldiers during the American Civil War, but these cocktails are named because, traditionally, the bourbon used in their making is a brand known as Rebel Yell.

Ingredients:

ice cubes
1½ measures bourbon
(Rebel Yell if available)
½ measure sherry
1 teaspoon Campari
3 measures mandarin juice
3 measures lemonade

Whisky

Method:

Half-fill the shaker with ice cubes.
Pour in the Campari, sherry, bourbon, and mandarin juice. Shake well, strain into an ice-filled Collins glass, and top with lemonade.

Method: SHAKER

Glass: COCKTAIL

Scots Guard

As the name suggests, this cocktail should be made with Scotch whisky.

Ingredients:

ice cubes

2 measures Scotch whisky

1 measure lemon juice

1 measure orange juice

½ teaspoon grenadine

Whisky

Method:

Half-fill the shaker with ice cubes.

Pour in the lemon and orange juice.

Add the grenadine and the whisky and shake well.

Strain and pour into a cocktail glass.

Southern Delta

*Southern Comfort lends its distinctive peach flavor
to this delight.*

Ingredients:

broken ice
1½ measures bourbon
½ measure Southern Comfort
⅓ measure lime juice
⅓ measure pineapple juice

Whisky

Method:

Put a glassful of broken ice in
the shaker.
Pour in the pineapple juice,
lime juice, Southern Comfort,
and the bourbon.
Shake well and pour
unstrained into an old-
fashioned glass.

Suburban

Leave the city behind and head for the "'burbs."

Ingredients:

ice cubes
broken ice
3 measures Scotch or bourbon
1 measure port
1 measure dark rum
3 drops bitters

Whisky

Method:

Half-fill the mixing glass with ice cubes.

Pour in the rum, port, whisky, and add the bitters.

Stir well and strain into an old-fashioned glass half-filled with broken ice.

The Sour

The original sour of the 1850s was the brandy sour,
but since then sours have been made with practically every
base spirit available and the whisky sour is now one of the most
popular. It's called a sour because very little sweetener and a
relatively large amount of lemon juice is used. It's traditionally
served in a stemmed sour glass, although it can also be served in
an old-fashioned glass when the optional soda water is added.
While a sour should never taste sweet, do adjust the amount of
sugar to suit. If you ask for a whisky sour in a bar, don't forget to
specify which whisky or whiskey you want. You can also have gin
sour, vodka sour, tequila sour, rum sour, and brandy sour.

Ingredients:

ice cubes

2 measures whisky of choice

1 measure lemon juice

½ measure gomme syrup

Whisky

Method:

Half-fill the shaker with ice cubes.

Pour in the lemon juice and gomme syrup and add the whisky.

Shake well and strain into a sour glass.

If you want to add a dash of soda water, serve on the rocks in an old-fashioned glass.

Method: SHAKER

Glass: COCKTAIL

Strongarm

Oddly named, since this drink is oh-so very easy to lift to one's lips.

Ingredients:

ice cubes

2 measures Scotch

½ measure triple sec or
Cointreau

½ measure lemon juice

Whisky

Method:

Half-fill the shaker with ice
cubes.

Pour in the triple sec or
Cointreau and the Scotch
and shake well.

Strain into a cocktail glass.

Thunderclap

*Too many of these, and that's what a pin dropping
will sound like!*

Ingredients:

ice cubes

1½ measures whisky of choice

1 measure gin

1 measure brandy

Whisky

Method:

Half-fill the mixing glass with
ice cubes.

Pour in the brandy, gin, and
whisky and stir well.

Strain into a cocktail glass.

Method:	SHAKER
Glass:	COCKTAIL

Tiger Juice

Ingredients:

ice cubes
1½ measures whisky
1 measure orange juice
½ measure lemon juice

Whisky

Method:

Half-fill the mixing glass with ice cubes.
Pour in the lemon and orange juice and add the whisky.
Shake well and strain into a cocktail glass.

Ward Eight

*A slight variation on the whisky sour will result
in this classic. You can serve it either as a cocktail in such a
glass, or in a tall glass with broken ice and a dash of soda
water, some fruit to garnish and with
straws. Try it both ways –
the ingredients are
the same.*

Ingredients:

broken ice

2 measures whisky

¼ measure orange juice

½ measure lemon juice

¼ measure grenadine

sodawater

citrus fruit

Whisky

Method:

Put a glassful of broken ice
into the shaker.

Pour in the orange and
lemon juices, grenadine and
whisky.

Shake well and strain into a
cocktail glass or, as
illustrated, into a highball
glass two-thirds filled with
broken ice and top with soda
water. Garnish with citrus
fruit.

method: SHAKER

glass: HIGHBALL

Whisky squirt

Squirts are sweet drinks made with a base spirit or wine in combination with fresh fruit.

Ingredients:

crushed ice

ice cubes

2 measures whisk(e)y

1 teaspoon triple sec or

Cointreau

½ measure gomme syrup

½ crushed fresh peach

(without skin)

2 measures soda water

Whisky

Method:

Crush the peach half in a
bowl or in a mixing glass.
Put a glassful of crushed ice
into the shaker.
Add the crushed peach, the
gomme syrup, triple sec or
Cointreau and whisky.
Shake well and then strain
over 3–4 ice cubes in a
highball glass.
Top up with soda water.
Serve with a straw.

Tequila cocktails

Margarita
see page 142.

The spirit of Mexico is made from the sap of the mezcal, also known as the century or argarth plant. It is not a cactus, but a type of aloe (related to the lily) of the genus *Agave*, specifically the blue-coloured *Agave tequilana weber*. There are over 120 types of agave, but only the blue agave, which grows in abundance around the town of Tequila in Jalisco state in Mexico, 65km (40 miles) west of Guadalajara, is used in tequila production. The manufacture of tequila is governed by strict quality standards. Mezcal, a much inferior form of tequila not subject to the same rigours, is produced in a number of regions from different varieties of agave.

Before the Conquistadors arrived in Mexico, the Aztecs had been happily drinking a low-alcohol wine made from the agave plant called pulque. This is still drunk in Mexico today. In the 16th century, the Spaniards imported the arts of distillation and tequila was born. It take between eight and ten years for an agave plant to grow to maturity, when it resembles a pineapple and is called a *pina* (the Spanish word for pineapple). The base of a mature agave plant is steamed to release the sap. The sap is then fermented for around ten days to make the 'mother pulque'. This is then added to fresh sap and allowed to ferment to produce the pulque wine. To make tequila, the pulque is double-distilled in pot stills.

It took a long time for tequila to cross the border into the United States, however. The first recorded shipment of just three barrels was in 1873. More Americans discovered the taste when US troops pursued Pancho Villa along the Mexican–American border in 1916, and by the time Prohibition kicked in, tequila had established a following. One of the mixed drinks that become popular in the 1930s was the tequila sunrise. In 1944 a 'gin famine' struck the United States and considerable amounts of tequila were imported to use as the base for cocktails. Tequila gained in popularity in the 1950s and by the 1960s had something of a cult status, particularly with students in California, who erroneously believed that tequila contained the hallucinogenic drug mescaline.

Nevertheless, tequila is a relative newcomer to the cocktail circuit, and is still the subject of experimentation among bartenders and adventurous drinkers. It certainly quickly acquired a number of drinking rituals and many a party-goer has lived to regret that final tequila slammer pressed upon them by enthusiastic friends. Stories about worms in tequila bottles are greatly exaggerated.

Despite Mexican government rules regarding the production of tequila, there are no laws governing how it is aged. Tequila Añejo simply means 'aged tequila', and it must be aged for one year in white-oak casks. Most producers claim that gold tequila has been aged in white-oak casks for between two and four years (rarely more than five years, as there is no improvement in flavour). silver tequila is aged in wax-lined vats and is more mellow than ordinary, 'white' tequila, although it, too, has no colour.

You either love it or hate it, but there is no mistaking the hydrogen sulphide odour (or rotten-egg smell) of neat tequila. Get past that and wait as the warm glow grows out from your stomach and travels south, right down to your toes!

Viva Mexico!

Tequila sunrise
see page 154.

Ambassador

A very simple drink to make, and a very refreshing one too!

Ingredients:

ice cubes
2 measures tequila
2–4 measures (or more)
orange juice
dash of gomme syrup
1 orange slice

Tequila

Method:

Put some ice cubes in the mixing glass.
Add the orange juice, gomme syrup and tequila.
Stir and pour over ice cubes in an old-fashioned glass.
Decorate with the orange slice.

Variation:

If you prefer a longer drink, add more orange juice and serve in a Collins glass.

method:	SHAKER
glass:	OLD FASHIONED
garnish:	APPLE WEDGE

Chimayo cocktail

Try this combination of tequila and apple juice.

Ingredients:

ice cubes

1½ measures tequila

½ measure lime juice

½ measure apple juice

apple wedge

Tequila

Method:

Place some ice cubes in the shaker.

Add the lime juice, apple juice and tequila and shake well.

Strain into an ice-filled old-fashioned glass and garnish with the apple wedge.

Border crossing

Mexico meets America in this tequila-cola blend.

Ingredients:

ice cubes

1½ measures tequila

2 teaspoons lime juice

1 teaspoon lemon juice

4 measures cola

1 lime wedge

Tequila

Method:

Almost fill a highball glass
with ice cubes.
Pour over the lime juice,
lemon juice and tequila and
top with cola.
Stir well and garnish with the
lime wedge.

method:	MIXING GLASS
glass:	COCKTAIL
garnish:	MARASCHINO CHERRY

California dream

Ingredients:

ice cubes

2 measures tequila

1 measure rosso vermouth

½ measure dry vermouth

1 maraschino cherry

Tequila

Method:

Half-fill the mixing glass with ice cubes.

Pour on the rosso vermouth, dry vermouth and tequila.

Stir well, strain into a cocktail glass and garnish with the maraschino cherry.

Doralto

Ingredients:

ice cubes
1½ measures tequila
½ measure lemon juice
½ teaspoon castor sugar
1 dash bitters
4 measures tonic water
1 lime slice

Tequila

Method:

Put some ice cubes in the shaker and pour in the lemon juice, sugar, dash of bitters and the tequila.

Shake well and strain into a highball glass two-thirds filled with ice cubes.

Top with the tonic water and garnish with the lime slice.

method:	SHAKER
glass:	OLD FASHIONED
garnish:	MARASCHINO CHERRY

Fruits of the desert

A delicious grapefruit flavour, softened by the addition of the orange-flavoured triple sec. Try it with 'gold' tequila – aged for between two and four years.

Ingredients:

ice cubes
broken ice
1½ measures tequila
(gold tequila if preferred)
½ measure triple sec or
Cointreau
2 measures grapefruit juice
1 teaspoon castor
sugar
1 maraschino cherry

Tequila

Method:

Half-fill the shaker with
ice cubes.
Pour in the grapefruit
juice, triple sec or
Cointreau, tequila and
add the sugar.
Shake well and strain into
an old-fashioned glass half
filled with broken ice.
Garnish with the maraschino
cherry.

El Dorado

*The legendary city of gold sought
by the Spanish explorers
in South America gives its name
to this drink. It's also a great honey
and vitamin C 'health drink'. But
if you believe that, then you really do
believe in fairy tales!*

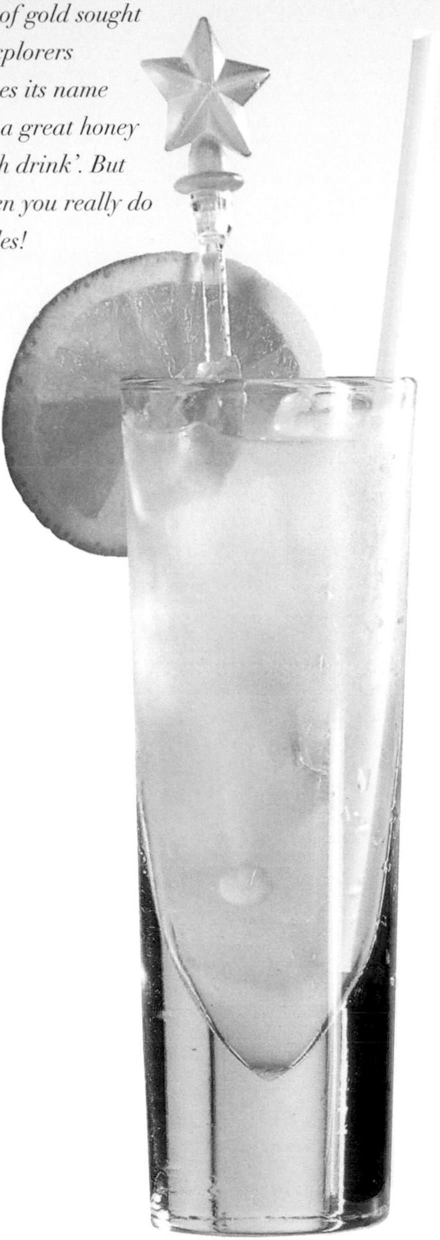

Ingredients:

ice cubes
2 measures tequila
1½ measures lemon juice
1 tablespoon clear honey
(about ½ measure)
1 orange slice

Tequila

Method:

Half-fill the shaker with ice
cubes.
Pour in the lemon juice,
honey and tequila and shake
vigorously. (That's the
aerobic-exercise part!)
Strain into a Collins glass
filled with ice cubes and
garnish with the orange slice.

method: BUILD
glass: HIGHBALL

Gentle Ben

Don't be fooled by the name: tequila, vodka and gin pack a real punch. Best drunk through a straw while lying in a hammock.

Ingredients:

ice cubes
1½ measures tequila
½ measure vodka
½ measure gin
4 measures orange juice

Tequila

Method:

Fill a highball glass two-thirds full of ice cubes.
Pour over the orange juice, gin, vodka and tequila and stir well.

Icebreaker

A relative of the Daiquiri, you can make this tequila drink in a blender or food processor.

Ingredients:

crushed ice

2 measures tequila

2 measures grapefruit juice

½ measure grenadine

2 teaspoons triple sec or
Cointreau

Tequila

Method:

Put about a glassful of
crushed ice in the blender.
Pour on the tequila, grapefruit
juice, grenadine and triple sec
or Cointreau.
Blend at low speed for about
12 to 15 seconds.
Strain into the sour glass and
serve straight up.

method:	SHAKER
glass:	TRADITIONALLY, A CHAMPAGNE SAUCER
garnish:	WEDGE OF LIME

Margarita

This is one of the best-known tequila-based drinks and also one of the most popular. Many young women called Margarita have claimed to be the inspiration for the drink, but most now accept that the muse was not, in fact, a Mexican señorita, but the American actress Marjorie King. Marjorie was a guest at Danny Herrera's Rancho La Gloria in Tijuana in 1948, when he discovered that the actress was allergic to every spirit except tequila. Herrera mixed this drink for her and named it Margarita, the Spanish for Marjorie. Since then, the Margarita has evolved from the original classic recipe into frozen versions and frozen fruit Margaritas which use fruit liqueurs.

Ingredients:

ice cubes
2 measures tequila
1¼ measures triple sec
or Cointreau
¾ measure lime juice
(or lemon if preferred)
limewedge

Tequila

Method:

Rub the rim of the glass with a wedge of lime and dip the rim into a saucer of salt.
Half-fill the shaker with ice cubes.
Pour in the lime juice, triple sec or Cointreau and tequila.
Shake well and strain into the champagne saucer.
Garnish with a wedge of lime on the edge of the glass.

Massacre

Ginger ale is a popular mixer with tequila and is the mixer for the infamous tequila slammer – known in France as tequila rapido and in Germany as tequila boom-boom. The slammer is not so much a drink as a 'method' of drinking: 1 measure of tequila and 1 measure ginger ale in a shot glass covered with one hand or a beer mat, banged twice on the table and downed in one. Someone even had the nerve to use champagne instead of ginger ale and created the slammer royale! Why have a slammer when you can have a massacre instead?

Tequila

Ingredients:

ice cubes
2 measures tequila
1 teaspoon Campari
4 measures ginger ale

Method:

Almost fill a highball glass with ice cubes, add the tequila and Campari. Top with ginger ale and stir well.

method:	SHAKER
glass:	COCKTAIL

Mexicano

The pineapple juice makes tequila go down nice and smoothly.

Ingredients:
ice cubes
2 measures tequila
1 measure pineapple juice
1 teaspoon grenadine
½ measure lemon juice

Tequila

Method:
Half-fill the shaker with ice cubes.
Pour in the lemon juice, grenadine and tequila and shake well.
Strain into a cocktail glass.

Mexican itch

*If you've got an itch, you just have to scratch it.
This is tequila the Mexican way. Again, it's not really a cocktail or
even a mixed drink, but a way of coming to terms with the often
ripe odour of neat tequila prior to swallowing it. It's sometimes
called a tequila cruda or a tequila shot.*

Ingredients:

1 measure tequila
1 small pinch of salt
1 wedge of lime

Tequila

Method:

Rub the lime wedge on your hand where your thumb and index finger meet.
Sprinkle the salt on this now wet part of your anatomy.
Hold the lime wedge between your thumb and index finger.
Hold the shot glass with the tequila in your other hand.
Take a deep breath and lick the salt off your hand.
Down the tequila in one swallow.
Bite on the lime wedge.

method:	SHAKER
glass:	OLD FASHIONED
garnish:	RED PEPPER

Ingredients:

ice cubes

broken ice

1 measure tequila

1 measure triple sec

or Cointreau

1 teaspoon pepper vodka

(see page **87** for how to

make your own)

1 measure orange juice

1 measure cranberry juice

1 hot red pepper

Pepper-eater

The trouble with tequila is that it brings out the
dare-devil in quite the most innocent of people.
Will you dare eat the red-pepper garnish?

Tequila

Method:

Half-fill the shaker
with ice cubes.
Pour in the tequila,
triple sec or Cointreau,
pepper vodka, orange
juice and cranberry juice.
Shake well and strain into
an old-fashioned glass
three-quarters filled with
broken ice.
Garnish with the red pepper.
Take bets on who will eat
their garnish.

Poker face

A nice, long drink that does allow you to keep a straight face – even if it's only for a short while!

Ingredients:

ice cubes
1 measure tequila
½ measure triple sec or
Cointreau
4 measures pineapple juice
1 lime wedge

Tequila

Method:

Almost fill a highball glass
with ice cubes.
Pour on the pineapple juice,
triple sec or Cointreau and
tequila.
Stir well and garnish with the
lime wedge.

method:	SHAKER
glass:	OLD FASHIONED
garnish:	MARASCHINO CHERRY ON A STICK

Purple cactus

This drink uses passionfruit juice – a pleasant change and a lovely flavour.

Ingredients:

ice cubes
broken ice
1½ measures tequila
1½ measures passionfruit juice
½ measure sherry
1 teaspoon grenadine
1 maraschino cherry on a stick

Tequila

Method:

Half-fill the shaker with ice cubes.
Add the tequila, passionfruit juice, sherry and grenadine. Shake well and strain into an old-fashioned glass three-quarters filled with broken ice.
Garnish with the cherry on a stick.

Variations:

Replace the tequila with koniak (Greek brandy) for a purple lizard or with Wild Turkey (straight bourbon) for a purple turkey.

Ridley

This drink was invented in London at the Duke's Hotel in around 1960. The addition of Galliano gives a subtle aniseed flavour to the drink.

Ingredients:

ice cubes

crushed ice

1 measure tequila

1 measure gin

1 teaspoon Galliano

1 orange slice

1 maraschino cherry

Tequila

Method:

Half-fill the shaker with ice cubes.

Pour in the tequila and gin and shake well.

Strain into the champagne saucer filled with crushed ice.

Sprinkle the Galliano on top and garnish with an orange slice and a cherry.

method:	BUILD
glass:	HIGHBALL
garnish:	LEMON TWIST

Rosita

The Campari and sweet vermouth make the pink colour of this 'little rose'.

Ingredients:

crushed ice

1½ measures tequila

1 measure Campari

½ measure rosso vermouth

½ measure dry vermouth

1 dash bitters

1 lemon twist

Tequila

Method:

Almost fill a highball glass with crushed ice.

Pour in the tequila, Campari, rosso and dry vermouths and add the dash of bitters.

Stir well and add the twist of lemon.

Scottie was beamed up

Star Trek fans will no doubt understand the significance of the name!

Ingredients:

ice cubes
2 measures tequila
½ measure Galliano

Tequila

Method:

Half-fill the mixing glass with ice cubes.
Pour in the tequila and Galliano and stir.
Strain into a cocktail glass.

method:	BUILD
glass:	OLD FASHIONED

Spanish fly

This almond-flavoured drink should not be confused with the infamous 'Spanish fly' (Lytta vascatoria), found in abundance in Spain and powdered to make the dubious aphrodisiac of the same name.

Ingredients:

broken ice
1½ measures tequila (gold tequila if possible)
½ measure sherry

Tequila

Method:

Fill an old-fashioned glass with broken ice. Add the tequila and the sherry and serve with a stirrer.

Submarino

This is a must for anyone who likes beer! Try the tequila
moonrise (page 155) as well. No tequila and no Mexican beer?
Then make a dog's nose: pour 1 measure of gin into
the beer of your choice.

Ingredients:
1 measure tequila
1 glass Mexican beer

Tequila

Method:
Pour the beer into the glass
and add the tequila!

method:	BUILD
glass:	HIGHBALL (ON THE ROCKS)
garnish:	ORANGE SLICE AND A CHERRY ON A STICK

Tequila sunrise

Created in Mexico in the 1930s, this long, beautifully coloured drink has remained incredibly popular – and even inspired a couple of songs! The ingredients are poured straight into the glass and the grenadine is allowed to sink to the bottom.

Ingredients:

ice cubes (if desired)

2 measures tequila

½ measure grenadine

4 measures orange juice

1 orange slice

1 maraschino cherry

Tequila

Method:

Pour the orange juice and tequila into the highball glass almost filled with ice cubes. Stir well and let it come to a rest.

Drop the grenadine into the centre of the drink and allow it to settle to the bottom. Garnish with the orange slice and cherry.

Variation:

Use 2 measures pineapple and 2 measures orange juice, and you'll enjoy a Florida sunrise.

Tequila moonrise

After the sun goes down, up comes the moon!

Ingredients:

ice cubes

3 measures tequila

I measure light rum

I measure dark rum

2 measures beer

½ measure Rose's Lime Juice

½ measure lemon juice

I teaspoon castor sugar

Tequila

Method:

Half-fill the shaker with ice cubes.

Pour in the tequila, light and dark rums, lime juice, lemon juice and the sugar.

Shake well and strain into a Collins glass half-filled with ice cubes.

Top up with the beer.

method: SHAKER

glass: COCKTAIL

Viva Villa

Francisco Doroteo Arango Villa, better known as the Mexican revolutionary general Pancho Villa (1877–1923) was, in fact, a well-known teetotaller. Perhaps then it's for fans of Aston Villa – although it's not in their club's colours!

Ingredients:

ice cubes
2 measures tequila
1 measure lime juice
1 teaspoon lemon juice
2 teaspoons castor sugar
1 lime wedge

Tequila

Method:

Place the sugar in a saucer. Rub the rim of the cocktail glass with the lime wedge and dip the rim into the sugar.

Discard the lime.

Half-fill the shaker with ice cubes and pour in the lemon juice, lime juice and tequila. Shake well and strain into the sugar-frosted cocktail glass.

Brandy cocktails

Any spirit distilled from fruit, rather than grain, is a brandy. The French term *eau-de-vie de vin* ('water of life from wine') is the generic term for all brandies. Good brandies come from France, Spain, Greece, Australia, South Africa, Portugal, the United States of America – wherever grapes are grown, brandy is made. Peru also produces a recently popular brandy called Pisco.

Only the spirit that is distilled in the registered district of France, however, has a right to be called cognac. The area is located north of Bordeaux and south of La Rochelle on the west coast of France and stretches inland to Angoulême. The river Charente runs through the region and gives its name to the two *départements* in which most of the vineyards are planted, the Charente and Charente-Maritime.

The boundaries of the area were set down in 1909, and because of the variations in the soil and consequently the quality of spirit produced, it was further subdivided into five 'divisions'. In the centre, around the town of Cognac itself, are the two finest areas of production, which account for around 21 per cent of cognac production: Grande Champagne and Petite Champagne. Next in quality is the cognac from Les Borderies, from the areas surrounding the Fine Champagne area, followed by that from Fins Bois and Bons Bois. Finally,

Horse's neck with a kick
see page 171.

production from the two outermost areas, Bois Ordinaires and Bois Cummuns, cannot be blended to make Grande or Fine Champagne, or, indeed, be added to the other three AOC (*Appellation d'Origine Contrôlé*) regions.

All cognac is made from wine that is fermented from whole grapes and then double-distilled in pot stills. It is then aged in new oak casks for one year and transferred to aged oak casks to stop the cognac from taking on too much tannin from the new oak. The labels on cognac bottles are designed to denote the quality of the spirit: V (Very), S (Special), O (Old), P (Pale), F (Fine), X (Extra), C (Cognac) and E (Especial). VO and VSOP mean that the cognac has been aged for at least 4½ years. The words Extra, Napoleon and Vieille Reserve are a government guarantee that the cognac has been aged at least 5½ years. The stars found on labels are also related to age: three-star cognac is the youngest, aged for a minimum of 18 months.

The second great *eau-de-vie de vin*, also from France, is armagnac, which is produced in Gascony, south of Bordeaux. While cognac is double-distilled in pot stills, armagnac is single-distilled in its own type of still and takes much of its flavour and colour from casks made of local oak, in which it matures.

Calvados is a brandy made from apples. A speciality of the Normandy region of northern France, Calvados is distilled from apple cider fermented for one month and then aged, sometimes for as long as 40 years. Calvados is known as *eau-de-vie de cidre* ('water of life from cider'). America also produces fine apple brandies known as applejack.

Other fruits are used to make *eau-de-vie* or brandy. The spirits are almost always colourless since they are bottled immediately after distillation to retain the fruit flavours and high alcohol content. The best known are Kirsch (made from cherries), Poire William (from pears), Mirabelle, Quetsch and Slivovitz (from different varieties of plums), Framboise (from raspberries), Prunelle (from sloe berries) and Fraises (from strawberries).

Mate
see page 173.

Betsy Ross

Named after Betsy Griscom Ross (1752–1836),
who made the very first United States flag

Ingredients:

ice cubes

2 measures brandy

1 measure port

½ teaspoon triple sec or

Cointreau

1 dash bitters

Brandy

Method:

Put some ice cubes in the
mixing glass and pour in the
brandy, port, triple sec or
Cointreau and bitters.
Stir well and strain into an
old-fashioned glass filled with
ice cubes.

method:	SHAKER
glass:	COCKTAIL
garnish:	TWIST OF LEMON (OPTIONAL)

Between the sheets

A perfect (and seductively named) after-dinner drink, this classic cocktail was created in the 1930s.

Ingredients:

ice cubes

1½ measures brandy

1 measure white rum

1 measure Cointreau

½ measure lemon juice

1 twist lemon (optional)

Brandy

Method:

Half-fill the shaker with ice cubes.

Pour in the brandy, rum, Cointreau and lemon juice and shake sharply.

Strain into a cocktail glass and garnish with the lemon twist (optional).

Burnt orange

Ingredients:

ice cubes

3 measures brandy

2 measures orange juice

3 drops bitters

Brandy

Method:

Put some ice cubes into the mixing glass and shake the bitters over the ice.
Pour in the orange juice and brandy and stir vigorously.
Strain into a cocktail glass.

method:	BUILD
glass:	COLLINS
garnish:	LONG SPIRAL OF ORANGE PEEL

Brandy cooler

A cooler is a long drink, similar to a Collins, but which usually contains a spiral of citrus peel trailing over the edge of the glass. It's also a little like a horse's neck (see page 171), but while that is made with ginger ale, the original Remsen cooler of the 1880s was made with soda water. The 19th-century fashion was for sweet coolers, sometimes topped with ice cream. Today, coolers are generally much drier and more thirst-quenching drinks, but you can sweeten yours according to taste.

Ingredients:

ice cubes
2 measures brandy
5 measures soda water
long spiral of lemon peel

Brandy

Method:

Decorate the Collins glass with the long spiral of peel so that it hangs over the side of the glass.
Place three or four ice cubes in the glass and pour in the brandy.
Add the soda and stir thoroughly.

Variations:

If you find it too dry, add a little sugar or try substituting a lemon-lime soda (such as 7-Up) for the plain soda water. Any base spirit can be used for a cooler.

Brandy Cuban

This is a little like the Cuba libre (page 60), but uses brandy in place of rum. A surprisingly good mix!

Ingredients:

ice cubes
2 measures brandy
1 measure lime juice
4 measures cold cola
1 slice lime

Brandy

Method:

Half-fill the highball glass with ice cubes.
Pour in the lime juice and brandy and top up with the cola.
Stir lightly and decorate with the lime slice.

method:	MIXING GLASS
glass:	COCKTAIL
garnish:	LEMON TWIST

Brandy perfect

Who are we to disagree?

Ingredients:

ice cubes

3 measures brandy

½ measure dry vermouth

½ measure rosso vermouth

1 lemon twist

Brandy

Method:

Place some ice cubes in the mixing glass and pour in the dry vermouth, rosso vermouth and the brandy. Stir vigorously and strain into the cocktail glass.

Add the twist of lemon and discard, or drop it into the glass if you wish.

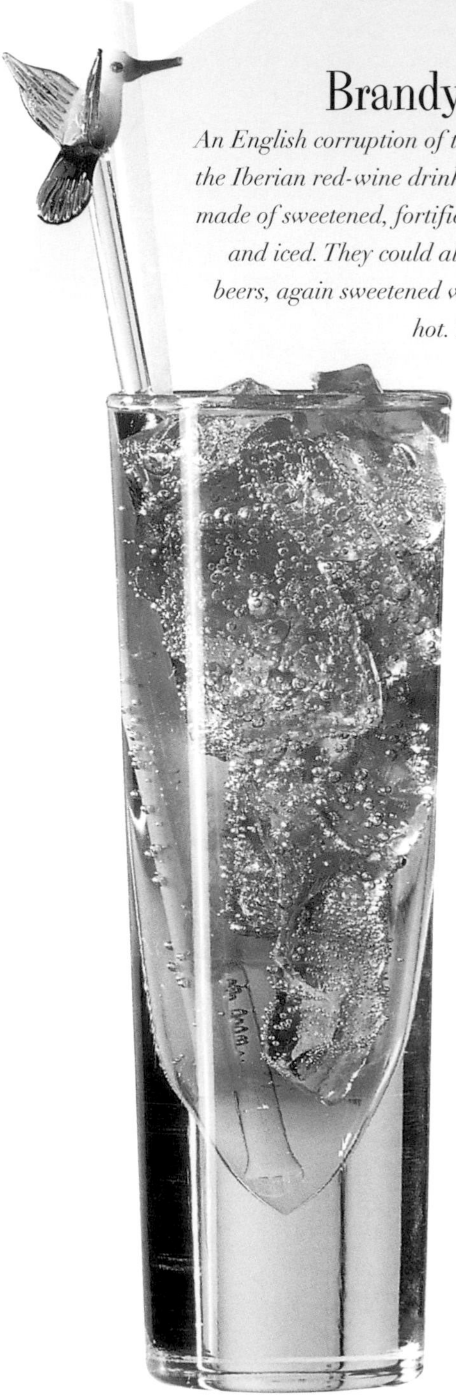

Brandy sangaree

*An English corruption of the Spanish word 'sangria',
the Iberian red-wine drink, sangarees were originally
made of sweetened, fortified wines served in a tumbler
and iced. They could also be made with ales and
beers, again sweetened with sugar, and often served
hot. This was done by heating a
poker in a fire until it
was red hot and then
immersing it in the
drink. Modern sangarees
use spirits and soda
water served in a
highball glass with a
traditional dusting of
nutmeg on the top.*

Ingredients:

broken ice
2½ measures brandy
½ measure port
½ measure gomme syrup
2½ measures soda water
grated nutmeg

Brandy

Method:

Fill a highball glass two-thirds
full with broken ice.
Pour in the brandy and the
gomme syrup.
Add the soda and float the
port on top.
Dust with the nutmeg and
add straws.

Variation:

Sangarees can be made
with any spirit: gin,
bourbon, whisky or
sherry can be used in
place of the brandy.

method:	BUILD
glass:	OLD FASHIONED
garnish:	SPRIG OF MINT

Brandy smash

*Smashes are drinks flavoured with crushed mint – a short version
of the mint julep (see page 117). Smashes first appeared in
America in the 1850s, and it is believed they took their name from
the fine smashed ice used to make them. Smashes can be made in
the same way with any spirit: replace the brandy with two
measures of either vodka, gin, rum, Scotch, rye or bourbon.*

Ingredients:

crushed ice

2 measures brandy

½ measure gomme syrup

2 sprigs mint

1 mint sprig for garnish

Brandy

Method:

Drop the two sprigs of mint
into the old-fashioned glass.
Pour in the gomme syrup and
gently crush the mint with a
muddler.

Add the brandy and then fill
the glass with the crushed
ice.

Garnish with the sprig of
mint and serve with a
muddler and straws.

Charles cocktail

Ingredients:
ice cubes
2 measures brandy
½ measure rosso vermouth
2 dashes bitters

Brandy

Method:
Put some ice cubes in the mixing glass and pour in the rosso vermouth and brandy. Add the bitters and stir well. Strain into a cocktail glass.

method:	SHAKER
glass:	COCKTAIL

City slicker

For when you've closed the big deal!

Ingredients:

ice cubes

2 measures brandy

½ measure triple sec or
Cointreau

½ measure lemon juice

Brandy

Method:

Half-fill the shaker with ice
cubes.

Pour in the brandy, triple sec
or Cointreau and lemon juice
and shake well.

Strain into a cocktail glass.

Comforting tiger

Drinks that contain the peach-, orange- and herb-flavoured bourbon, Southern Comfort (one of America's oldest liqueurs from St Louis, Missouri), often have 'comfort' or 'southern' in their names. See the slow comfortable screw (page 104) and the Southern delta (page 123).

Ingredients:

crushed ice
2 measures brandy
½ measure Southern Comfort
1 teaspoon rosso vermouth
1 lemon twist

Brandy

Method:

Half-fill the mixing glass with crushed ice.
Pour in the rosso vermouth, Southern Comfort and brandy and stir well.
Strain into a cocktail glass and garnish with the lemon twist.

method:	MIXING GLASS
glass:	COCKTAIL

Esquire

An elegant brandy and gin cocktail.

Ingredients:

ice cubes

2 measures brandy

1 measure gin

3 drops bitters

Brandy

Method:

Put some ice cubes into the mixing glass.

Shake the bitters over the ice and then pour in the gin and brandy.

Stir vigorously and strain into a chilled cocktail glass.

Horse's neck with a kick

The original horse's neck started life in the 1890s as a non-alcoholic mix of lemon peel, ice and ginger ale. By around 1910 it had become a whisky drink and Scotch, Irish, rye or bourbon was used as requested. This became known as a 'stiff horse's neck'. With Prohibition, the horse's neck reverted to its 'plain' formula – although speakeasies might add some bath-tub gin. Now the horse's neck with a kick is made with either brandy or bourbon and is usually served like a cooler – with a long spiral of citrus peel.

Ingredients:

ice cubes

2 measures brandy

1 dash bitters

4 measures ginger ale

1 lemon-peel spiral

Brandy

Method:

Cut a long spiral of lemon peel and hang it over the highball glass.

Half-fill the glass with ice cubes and pour in the brandy. Add the bitters and top with ginger ale.

method:	MIXING GLASS
glass:	COCKTAIL/LINE
garnish:	TWIST OF LEMON

Lord Chamberlain

Ingredients:

ice cubes

2 measures brandy

1 measure port

1 measure dry vermouth

3 drops bitters

1 lemon twist

Brandy

Method:

Put some ice cubes in the mixing glass and pour the vermouth and port over the ice.

Add the bitters and then pour in the brandy.

Stir well and then strain into a chilled cocktail glass.

Add the twist of lemon.

Mate

Ingredients:

ice cubes
3 measures brandy
1 measure dry vermouth
1 measure orange juice
½ teaspoon grenadine

Brandy

Method:

Put some ice cubes into the mixing glass and pour in the orange juice, grenadine, vermouth and brandy.
Stir until the mix becomes frothy and then strain into a sour or white-wine glass.

Metropolitan

For the man – or woman – about town.

Ingredients:

crushed ice
2 measures brandy
½ measure rosso vermouth
1 teaspoon castor sugar
1 dash bitters

Brandy

Method:

Half-fill the shaker with
crushed ice.
Pour in the rosso vermouth,
sugar, dash of bitters and the
brandy.
Shake well.
Strain into a cocktail glass.

Montana

A taste as big as the state, and an interesting presentation.

Ingredients:

ice cubes

2 measures brandy

2 teaspoons port

2 teaspoons dry vermouth

Brandy

Method:

Put some ice cubes in the mixing glass and pour in the brandy, port and vermouth. Strain into a cocktail glass with a single ice cube in it.

method:	MIXING GLASS
glass:	COCKTAIL

Monte rosa

This lime-flavour cocktail was invented in the 1920s. Originally it was served 'straight up' without the sugar. It is also sometimes served in an old-fashioned glass filled with broken ice. Try the variations for yourself.

Ingredients:

ice cubes

3 measures brandy

1 measure Cointreau

½ measure lime juice

Brandy

Method:

Put some ice cubes in the mixing glass and pour in the lime juice.

Add the Cointreau and brandy and stir well.

Strain into a chilled cocktail glass.

method:	MIXING GLASS
glass:	SOUR (OR WHITE-WINE GLASS)

Robinson

A drink for when you're cast away on a desert island! (With a well-stocked bar, you might not want to be rescued).

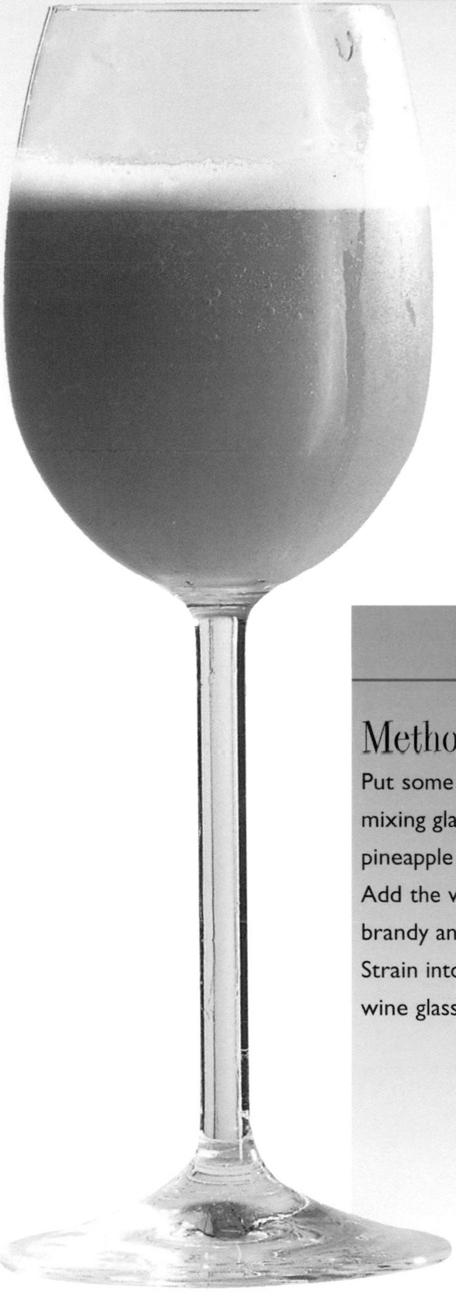

Ingredients:

ice cubes
3 measures brandy
1 measure dry vermouth
1 measure pineapple juice

Brandy

Method:

Put some ice cubes into the mixing glass and pour in the pineapple juice.
Add the vermouth and brandy and stir until frothy.
Strain into a sour or white-wine glass.

method:	SHAKER
glass:	OLD FASHIONED

Sidecar

*Created shortly after the First World War, at
Harry's Bar in Paris, this drink was named in
honour of the army captain who arrived at the
bar in a chauffeur-driven motorcycle sidecar.
Originally served in a champagne saucer, the
sidecar is now more often served over broken ice
in an old-fashioned glass.*

Ingredients:

ice cubes

broken ice

2 measures cognac (or armagnac)

1 measure Cointreau

1 measure lemon juice

Brandy

Method:

Half-fill the shaker with ice
cubes.

Pour in the lemon juice,
Cointreau and brandy and
shake well.

Strain into an old-fashioned
glass nearly filled with broken
ice.

Variations:

You can adjust the amount of lemon juice to suit. Add 1 measure of
white rum, and you'll have a Boston sidecar. If Calvados or applejack
(apple brandies) are used in place of the cognac, this is an applecart.
Replace the brandy with gin, and you have a Chelsea sidecar.

Star

This is possibly the best-tasting use of grapefruit juice yet!

Ingredients:

ice cubes

3 measures brandy

1 measure gin

1 measure grapefruit juice

½ teaspoon rosso vermouth

½ teaspoon dry vermouth

Brandy

Method:

Half-fill the shaker with ice cubes.

Pour in the grapefruit juice, vermouths, gin and brandy and shake well.

Strain into a cocktail glass.

method:	SHAKER
glass:	COCKTAIL
garnish:	MARASCHINO CHERRY

St Kitts

Named after the island of St Kitts in the Leeward Islands of the eastern West Indies.

Brandy

Method:

Half-fill the shaker with ice cubes.

Pour in the grapefruit juice, vermouth and brandy and shake well.

Strain into a cocktail glass and drop in the maraschino cherry.

Ingredients:

ice cubes

3 measures brandy

1 measure dry vermouth

1½ measures grapefruit juice

1 maraschino cherry

Tantalus cocktail

The son of the god Zeus and king of Sipylos in ancient Lydia, Tantalus is remembered for his punishment in Hades for having stolen ambrosia, the food of the gods. For his crime, Tantalus stood in water up to his chin and was 'tantalised' with food and drink, which moved out of his reach whenever he tried to satisfy his hunger and thirst. His name lives on in this equally tantalising cocktail (and in the lockable case for decanters of wines and spirits, a tantalus. The drink can be seen, but not enjoyed, except by the owner of the key).

Ingredients:

ice cubes
3 measures brandy
1 measure Cointreau
1 measure lemon juice

Brandy

Method:

Put some ice cubes in the mixing glass and pour in the lemon juice, Cointreau and brandy.
Stir vigorously and then strain into a cocktail glass.

Wine & Champagne cocktails

Wine can be divided into four categories: still wine; sparkling wine; fortified wine and aromatised wine, and the recipes that follow give you an opportunity to use all of them. There are three types of still wine: red, white and rosé. Each can also be dry, medium dry or sweet. For our purposes, wines will be mixed with other flavourings and liqueurs, so it would be sacrilege to use a very fine wine which is best enjoyed on its own.

The undoubted 'queen' of sparkling wines is, of course, champagne. To truly be called champagne, the wine must come from the designated region in France, 160km (100 miles) north of Paris, around Rheims and Épernay. However, other fine sparkling wines – what the French call *vins mousseux* and the Italians call *spumante* – are made outside the region and outside France. Champagne should be thoroughly chilled, but not icy. Gently ease the cork out – don't pop it! By all means use champagne for those special occasions, but try some of the great sparkling wines from California, Australia, Spain, Italy and France as well.

Fortified wines are wines which have had brandy added to them. Port and sherry are the two best-known types of fortified wines. Port comes from the Douro region of Portugal. The brandy added to the wine stops the process of fermentation,

Bellini
see page 188.

Black velvet
see page 189.

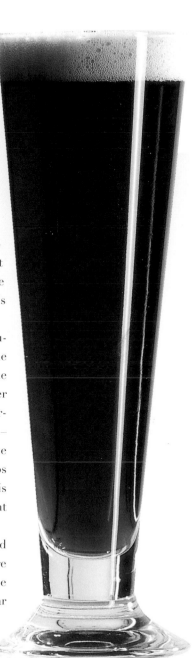

leaving some of the sugar behind and resulting in the sweet fortified wine. Vintage port has been declared by the maker as being good enough to be called vintage. It must be bottled within two years and then aged in the bottle for between 8 and 20 years. Tawny port is aged in the barrel and is clarified of sediment by using egg whites. Because it is barrel-aged, the wood takes out some of the colour of the port: the longer it is aged, the paler (tawnier) and drier the port becomes. Ruby port is aged for less time and consequently keeps some of its colour and its full body. White port is drier than the other ports and is made only from white grapes, although it is still barrel-aged. A good tawny port is perfect for making many of the mixed drinks offered here.

Sherry got its name simply because the English had trouble pronouncing the Spanish name Jerez, the town in the Cadiz region of Spain where sherry is made. It is only a true sherry if it is made in the Jerez region, although several other countries (such as South Africa and Cyprus) also produce versions. The wine is placed in casks in order for a yeast scum – called flor – to develop. This is caused by natural airborne yeast and growth is variable. The amount of flor that develops governs the type of sherry produced. At this point, the wine is fortified with brandy. Dry fino sherry makes an excellent mixed drink.

Aromatised wines were originally sour wines sweetened with honey and herbs to make them more palatable. They are generally quite sweet, with a high proportion of mistelle (brandy mixed with grape juice). Some of the most popular aromatised wines are Campari, and the aromatised wines – both dry and sweet – called vermouths.

Adonis

Named after the beautiful youth of Greek myth, Adonis was also the god of plants and vegetation. In ancient Athens, the midsummer festival the Adonia was celebrated in his honour with pots of bright summer flowers and herbs. This cocktail of sherry and vermouth captures in its flavours the herbs and wine of the island of Aphrodite.

Ingredients:

ice cubes

2 measures sherry

1 measure rosso vermouth

2 dashes bitters

Wine & Champagne

Method:

Put some ice cubes in the mixing glass and pour in the vermouth, bitters and the sherry. Stir well and strain into a cocktail glass.

American dream

*This is a fabulous red-wine drink and a refreshing
alternative to a 'straight' glass of red wine. Don't be alarmed by
the ingredients – it tastes fantastic!*

Ingredients:

ice cubes

3 measures red wine
(since it's an American
dream, try a Californian
wine)

⅓ measure bourbon

⅓ measure rosso vermouth

3 measures cold cola

1 slice orange

1 maraschino cherry

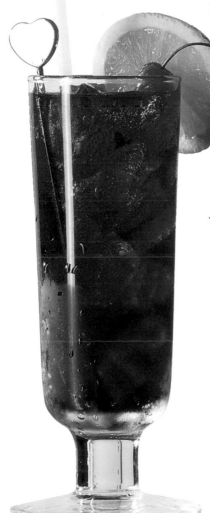

Wine & Champagne

Method:

Half-fill a highball glass with ice cubes.

Pour in the wine, vermouth, bourbon and top
with cold cola.

Stir gently and garnish with the orange slice
and the cherry.

Serve with a stirrer and straws.

method:	BUILD
glass:	HIGHBALL
garnish:	LEMON AND ORANGE TWISTS, SLICE OF ORANGE (OPTIONAL)

Americano

*One of the classic – and classiest – aperitifs of all time,
it is very simple to make well. It's a great drink to have while
indulging in that Italian pastime of 'people watching'.*

Ingredients:

ice cubes

1½ measures Campari

1½ measures rosso vermouth

soda water to taste

Wine & Champagne

Method:

Half-fill the highball glass with ice cubes.
Pour the vermouth and then the Campari
into the glass.

Add the twists of lemon and orange.

Stir well.

Decorate with the slice of orange.

Add soda water (optional) to taste – the soda
water gives the drink its freshness.

Sit back and watch the world go by!

Bamboo

This cocktail is not only a great aperitif, but tastes wonderful with Chinese or Thai food. The colder the mixing glass and the colder the cocktail glass, the better.

Ingredients:

1½ measures sherry

1½ measures dry vermouth

1–2 dashes bitters

1 twist lemon

Wine & Champagne

Method:

Make sure the mixing glass is really cold — swill a few ice cubes around first.

Get rid of any melted water by straining the cubes and then return them to the mixing glass.

Pour the sherry and vermouth over the ice and stir well for a few seconds.

Strain and serve in a well-chilled cocktail glass with a twist of lemon.

method:	BUILD
glass:	CHAMPAGNE FLUTE
garnish:	SEASONAL FRUIT (OPTIONAL)

Bellini

In 1943, Venice honoured one of its most famous sons, the Renaissance painter Giovanni Bellini (c. 1430–1516) with a major exhibition of his works. At Harry's Bar in Venice, legendary bartender Guiseppe Cipriani marked the occasion by creating this champagne and peach-juice cocktail.

Ingredients:

3 measures champagne – thoroughly chilled

1 large peach, skinned and puréed to make 1½ measures peach juice

1 teaspoon gomme syrup

Wine & Champagne

Method:

Remove the skin from the peach and purée it in a blender or food processor. You should have enough puree for 1½ measures.

Pour the peach purée/juice into the chilled champagne flute and add the gomme syrup.

Pour in the extremely well-chilled champagne. Decorate with garnish if desired.

variation:

Try a Mango Bellini: use 1½ measures of mango juice instead of the peach juice.

Black velvet
(also known as Bismarck)

This very chic-looking champagne and stout drink was created in 1861 at Brook's Club in London. Prince Albert, husband of Queen Victoria, had died and England was in mourning. At Brook's it was decided that even the champagne should pay its respects and it, too, went into mourning black by being mixed with Guinness. The Black velvet became an immensely popular drink and was the favourite tipple of Prince Otto von Bismarck, Chancellor of Germany, hence its alternative name.

Ingredients:

Chilled stout
Chilled champagne

Wine & Champagne

Method:

Chill the stout and the champagne.
Half-fill a glass with stout (Guinness, Murphy or Beamish).
Gently fill the glass with the chilled champagne.

variations:

A lager-champagne is called a Halsted Street Special.

If you don't want to use champagne, try a very dry, sparkling white wine instead.

method:	SHAKER
glass:	COLLINS
garnish:	SEASONAL FRUIT

Camp Grenada

A clever mix of Campari and grenadine.

Ingredients:

ice cubes

1½ measures Campari

½ measure grenadine

2 measures grapefruit juice

1 measure pineapple juice

3 measures cold lemon-lime

soda (e.g., 7-Up)

seasonal fruit

Wine & Champagne

Method:

Half-fill the shaker with ice cubes.

Pour in the grapefruit and pineapple juices.

Add the grenadine and Campari and shake
well.

Strain into an ice-filled Collins glass and top
with the lemon-lime soda.

Garnish with the seasonal fruit.

Champagne cocktail

The ultimate cocktail – when absolutely nothing else will do.
The champagne cocktail was the result of a cocktail competition
held in New York in 1889. The first prize, a gold medal, was
awarded to John Dougherty for his recipe – although he had, in
fact, discovered it 25 year earlier in the southern states of America.

Ingredients:

3 measures well-chilled champagne
⅓ measure cognac (brandy will
be OK, but only just!)
1 sugar cube
2 dashes bitters
1 twist lemon
½ orange slice

Wine & Champagne

Method:

Drop the sugar cube into the champagne
flute.
Add the bitters so that the sugar cubes soaks
them up.
Pour in the cognac and then fill the flute with
the chilled champagne.
Squeeze the twist of lemon and discard.
Decorate with the half slice of orange.

method:	MIXING GLASS
glass:	COCKTAIL
garnish:	2 MARASCHINO CHERRIES ON A STICK

Crimean cocktail

You'll need a fine sieve for this cocktail.

Ingredients:

ice cubes

2 measures dry white wine

⅔ measure Cointreau

grated zest of 1 lemon

1 measure soda water

2 maraschino cherries

Wine & Champagne

Method:

Put 3–4 ice cubes into the mixing glass and pour in the white wine and Cointreau.

Add the lemon zest and stir well.

Strain through a fine sieve into a cocktail glass.

Add the soda and garnish with the two cherries.

Diablo

We've already 'conjured up' a rum Diabolo (see page 63),
and now's the chance to prove that port is not just for old men or
to drink with Stilton cheese. The Diablo is also an opportunity to
use white port – a drink that is too often overlooked.

Ingredients:

ice cubes

2 measures dry white port

1½ measures rosso vermouth

a few drops of lemon juice

Wine & Champagne

Method:

Half-fill the shaker with ice cubes.
Pour in the vermouth and the port and
squeeze in a few drops of lemon juice.
Shake well and strain into a cocktail glass.

method:	BUILD
glass:	BALLON OR LARGE WINE GLASS
garnish:	SLICE OF ORANGE

Diplomatic answer

This is a great herb- and orange-flavoured long drink based on vermouth and brandy. Vermouth is generally considered an aperitif, while brandy is a digestif. The diplomatic answer – combining the two – means you really can drink this at any time.

Ingredients:

broken ice

2 measures rosso vermouth

1 measure brandy

⅓ measure triple sec or

Cointreau

4 measures lemonade

slice of orange

Wine & Champagne

Method:

Half-fill a large wine glass with broken ice.
Pour in the vermouth, brandy and triple sec
or Cointreau and top with lemonade.
Garnish with the slice of orange.

First Avenue

Avenues are short drinks based on sherry and built in a glass which has been chilled enough to have an ice frosting. The First Avenue uses Cointreau, but any fruit liqueur can be used – but only enough so that it makes a subtle contribution to the overall flavour.

Ingredients:

broken ice

1½ measures sherry

½ measure Cointreau

¾ measure soda water

1 teaspoon Campari

Wine & Champagne

Method:

Fill an old-fashioned glass two-thirds full with broken ice.

Pour in the sherry, Cointreau, Campari and soda.

196

method:	BUILD
glass:	COLLINS
garnish:	½ SLICE OF LEMON AND A CHERRY

French 75

The original '75 cocktail' was created during the First World War in Paris by Henry at Henry's Bar, and was named in honour of the French 75 light field gun. Post-war, Harry MacElhone, at Harry's Bar in Paris, added champagne and renamed it the French 75. By 1930 it was incredibly popular and spawned a whole number of Frenches – the 25, 45, 65, 95 and the 125.

Vive la France!

Ingredients:

ice cubes
5 measures well-chilled champagne
1 measure gin
1 measure lemon juice
1 heaped teaspoon castor sugar
½ lemon slice
1 maraschino cherry

Wine & Champagne

Method:

Pour the gin and lemon juice into the Collins glass.
Add the sugar and make sure it dissolves.
Fill the glass two-thirds full with ice and add the champagne.
Garnish with ½ a lemon slice and a maraschino cherry and serve with straws.

Variations:

Practice your French:
FRENCH 25: 5 measures champagne, 1 measure tequila, 1 measure lemon juice, ½ measure maple syrup.
FRENCH 45: a French 75 with Drambuie instead of gin and only ½ teaspoon sugar.
FRENCH 65: a French 75 with 2 teaspoons brandy floated on top.
FRENCH 95: a French 75 with bourbon instead of gin.
FRENCH 125: a French 75 with cognac instead of gin.

Hillary Wallbanger

Meet Harvey's cousin!

Ingredients:

ice cubes

4 measures dry white wine

2 measures orange juice

½ measure Galliano

Wine & Champagne

Method:

Fill the Collins glass two-thirds full with ice cubes.

Pour in the white wine and orange juice and stir well.

Float the Galliano on top.

method:	BUILD
glass:	CHAMPAGNE FLUTE

Mimosa

There is often a little confusion surrounding the mimosa and its close relative, the buck's fizz. A mimosa is simply a delicious 50:50 mix of champagne and orange juice created in 1925 at the Ritz Hotel in Paris and named after the beautiful tropical flower whose colour it resembles.

Ingredients:

3 measures chilled
champagne
3 measures orange juice
1 twist orange

Wine & Champagne

Method:

Pour the chilled orange juice and champagne into the well-chilled flute. Add the twist of orange.
Add ½ measure Cointreau and you have a grand mimosa.

The buck's fizz is the mimosa's older sister – created in 1921 in London at the Buck's Club. It differs from the mimosa in both the ratio of orange juice to champagne and in the inclusion of grenadine.

Negroni

A perfect balance of sweetness and bitterness, the Negroni is named after the Florentine Count Camillo Negroni. The drink was created in 1919 at the Casoni Bar in Florence, where the count usually ordered an Americano. One day, however, he asked for a little gin to be added to his drink and the result was the immensely popular Negroni.

Ingredients:

ice cubes
1 measure Campari
1 measure rosso vermouth
1 measure gin
soda water (optional)
slice of orange

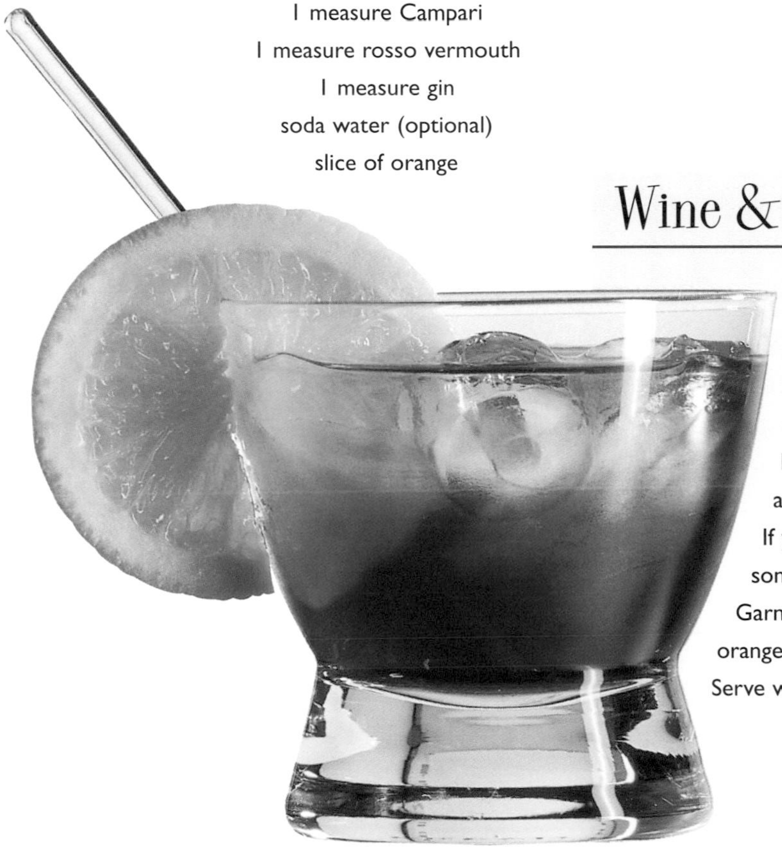

Wine & Champagne

Method:

Almost fill an old-fashioned glass with ice cubes.
Pour in the gin, vermouth and sherry and stir.
If you want a long drink, add some soda.
Garnish with the slice of orange.
Serve with a stirrer.

method: BUILD

glass: BALLON

Night and day

'Night and day, you are the one,
Only you beneath the moon and under the sun.'
Cole Porter, 'Night and Day' from
Gay Divorce (1932).

Ingredients:

crushed ice

3 measures champagne

¾ measure cognac

½ measure Cointreau

¼ measure Campari

Wine & Champagne

Method:

Half-fill a ballon with crushed ice.

Pour in the cognac, Cointreau and Campari.

Add the chilled champagne.

Operator

A great ginger-wine flavour!

Ingredients:

2 measures cold, dry white wine

2 measures dry ginger ale

1 teaspoon lime juice

1 slice lime

Wine & Champagne

Method:

Put 3 or 4 ice cubes in an old-fashioned glass. Pour in the wine.

Add the lime juice and the dry ginger ale.

Ozone

Sit in the shade or wear a hat with this one!

Ingredients:

¾ measure sherry

¾ measure bourbon

1 measure pineapple juice

½ measure lime juice

1 teaspoon Campari

1 teaspoon grenadine

Wine & Champagne

Method:

Put a glassful of broken ice into the shaker.

Pour in the sherry, bourbon, lime juice, pineapple juice, Campari and grenadine. Shake well and then pour unstrained into an old-fashioned glass.

Quick thrill

If your host asks 'How about a quick thrill?'
– don't slap his face!

Ingredients:

ice cubes

3 measures red wine

⅓ measure dark rum

3 measures cold cola

Wine & Champagne

Method:

Put some ice cubes in the goblet or wine
glass and pour in the wine and rum.
Top with the cold cola and quiver with
delight!

Regatta

A great drink – perfect for Henley or even Cowes Week. Although it has a nautical name, there's not a drop of rum in sight!

Ingredients:

3 measures chilled champagne
½ measure Galliano
½ measure triple sec or Cointreau
½ measure lemon juice
1 teaspoon vodka

Wine & Champagne

Method:

Pour the Galliano, triple sec or Cointreau, lemon juice and vodka into a chilled champagne flute.
Add the chilled champagne.

Ritz Bar fizz

Created at the Ritz Bar of the Ritz-Carlton Hotel in Boston, Massachusetts.

Wine & Champagne

Ingredients:

3 measures chilled champagne
1 measure grapefruit juice
1 measure pineapple juice
1 teaspoon grenadine
1 maraschino cherry
1 sprig of mint

Method:

Pour the pineapple and grapefruit juices into a chilled champagne saucer.
Pour in the chilled champagne and add the grenadine.
Garnish with the sprig of mint and the cherry.

Punches, cups' & toddies

A punch is a spiced, alcoholic, mixed drink served to a number of people, usually from a bowl. The origins of the word punch are debatable. It may have derived from 'puncheon', a large beer cask that held 72 gallons, or perhaps from the Hindu word *paunch*, which means five. The latter explanation is often believed because a punch usually contains at least five ingredients

In the first half of the 17th century, punches were generally made with ale, brandy or wine. With the colonisation of Jamaica from 1655 onwards, the basis of many punches became rum. The simplest rum punch consists of rum, sugar, water and orange juice.

Party punches are great fun to make and drink. They should be served in a bowl with a large block of ice in it to keep it cool – ice cubes melt quickly and dilute the punch. You can make a block or brick of ice quite easily in a clean juice or milk carton. Alternatively, set the punch bowl on a large salver or serving dish and surround it with ice cubes.

Cups, such as the stirrup cup, are also made in large quan-

Manhattan punchtab
see page 225.

tities, and were traditionally offered to the members of a hunting party before 'the off'. Toddies, which are hot drinks, may have originated in the East Indies in the form of 'tarries', the 17th-century word for a drink made from fermented palm juice. Most toddies use Scotch whisky as their base, but they can be made with most spirits with a little sugar, some spices and a slice of citrus fruit. They are wonderful on cold evenings by the fireside, or if you feel a little under the weather. You will also find a couple of ideas for hot drinks based on coffee, cocoa and tea.

For hot drinks, make sure the glasses used are heat-proof and warm them before pouring in the liquids. Heat-proof glasses are available in a range of sizes and styles, from cups to goblets and tall glasses for Irish coffee. If you don't have these, don't worry: these hot drinks look and taste just as good in an attractive china mug or cup.

Take extra care with hot liquids, especially when igniting spirits!

English bishop
see page 216.

Alhambra (hot)

*This is so simple to make and so delicious: it's really for
grown-ups who never really grew up!*

Ingredients:

5 measures hot cocoa or drinking
chocolate, made how you like it best
1 measure cognac

Punches, cups & toddies

Method:

Pour the hot cocoa or drinking chocolate
into the warmed glass and add the cognac.

Boston punch (cold)

This is a wonderfully refreshing
apple-wine flavour punch.
It will serve around 15 people.

Ingredients:

block of ice
750 ml (1 bottle) champagne or sparkling
white wine
300 ml (10 fl oz) cider
150 ml (5 fl oz) brandy
2 measures triple sec or Cointreau
3 measures dark rum
4 measures lemon juice
400 ml (14 fl oz) sparkling mineral water
1 tablespoon sugar
apple wedges

Punches, cups & toddies

Method:

In the punch bowl, dissolve the sugar in the
lemon juice, rum and triple sec or Cointreau.
Add the block of ice to the bowl and pour in
the brandy and cider and then the mineral
water and champagne or sparkling wine.
Add thin wedges of apple.
To stop cut apple from turning brown, dip the
pieces in some lemon juice.

method:	SAUCEPAN
glass:	BEER MUG
garnish:	SLICE OF LEMON

Brown Betty (hot)

*This is a terrific, hot, beer-based punch. The quantities
given will serve around eight people.*

Ingredients:

4 x 12 oz bottles amber ale
(1.3 litres in total)

12 measures brandy

2¼ cups water

½ cup brown sugar

1 lemon, sliced

4 whole cloves

1 cinnamon stick

½ teaspoon grated nutmeg

¼ teaspoon ground ginger

Variations

Another version of the brown Betty uses
the juice of the lemon instead of slices and
the whole hot mix is poured over slices of
toasted raisin bread that has been dusted
with cinnamon and ginger.

Punches, cups & toddies

Method:

In a large saucepan, over a
medium heat, add the sugar,
lemon slices, cloves, cinnamon,
nutmeg, ginger and water. Stir
continuously to dissolve the
sugar and let the mixture
come to the boil. Turn the
heat down and let the
mixture simmer for around
10 minutes. Add the brandy
and the ale, then heat, but do
not boil. Serve hot in beer
mugs, each garnished with a
slice of lemon.

Bumpo (hot)

Ingredients:

2 measures hot water

2 measures rum

1 measure lime juice

1 teaspoon sugar

ground nutmeg

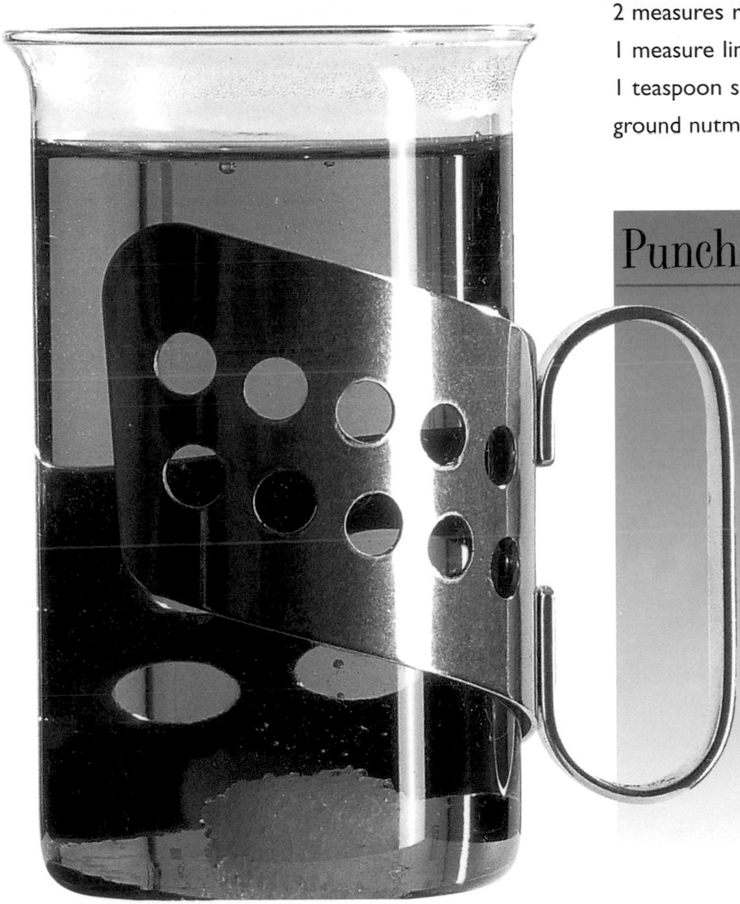

Punches, cups & toddies

Method:

Dissolve the sugar in the glass with the lime juice and hot water.

Add the rum and dust lightly with the ground nutmeg.

method:	SAUCEPAN AND LID
glass:	HEAT-PROOF CUP
garnish:	SUGAR-RIMMED CUP

Cafe d'Amour (hot)

This is a coffee made without cream – the perfect way to end
an intimate dîner à deux: It is, after all, the 'coffee of love'.
Be careful when you heat and ignite the cognac – the only thing
that should be inflamed are your passions, not the kitchen.

Ingredients:

5 measures hot black coffee

1¼ measures cognac

zest of ½ lemon

1 stick cinnamon

sugar (to rim the cup and to

sweeten, if desired)

Variation:

For a café brûlot, add one
clove and the zest of half an
orange to the saucepan
before heating. The cup in this
instance is not sugar-rimmed.

Punches, cups & toddies

Method:

Rim the cup with lemon and dip
into some sugar. Add the
coffee, lemon zest and the
cinnamon stick to the
saucepan and simmer.
Carefully pour the cognac into
a large soup ladle and ignite it.
Pour the flaming cognac into the
coffee and then extinguish the flame by
putting the lid on the saucepan. Remove
the lid and strain the mixture into the sugar-
rimmed cup.

Colonial boy (hot)

This is a wonderful, tea-based hot drink that's perfect after a long, winter walk.

Ingredients:

5 measures hot black tea
(sweetened to taste)
⅓ measure Irish whiskey
1 dash bitters

Variation:

For hot-T: omit the bitters and replace the whisky with 1
measure Cointreau. Add a slice of orange to garnish.
Try a fireside tea: combine in a glass 1 measure rum, 5
measures hot black tea, 1 wedge of lemon and 1 stick of
cinnamon.

Punches, cups & toddies

Method:

Pour the hot tea into the glass
and add the whiskey and bitters.

Confetti punch (cold)

A beautiful punch, perfect for a summer wedding.
The secret is to chill all the ingredients well in advance.
The recipe will serve about 40 people.

Ingredients:

700 ml (1¼ pints) white rum
1½ litres (2⅔ pints) champagne
or dry, sparkling wine
1 litre (1¾ pints) lemonade
700 ml (1¼ pints) white
grape juice
500 ml (18 fl oz) orange juice
1 punnet strawberries, halved

Punches, cups & toddies

Method:

Chill all the ingredients for at least two hours
– the longer the better.
Simply pour all the ingredients into the punch
bowl and stir gently.
Add the halved strawberries.
Serve in chilled ballon or wine glasses.

Dragoon punch (cold)

Try this punch when the cavalry arrives! For 12 people.

Ingredients:

block of ice
500 ml (1 pint) sherry
500 ml (1 pint) brandy
3 bottles or 1½ pints stout (850 ml)
3 bottles or 1½ pints lager (850 ml)
2 bottles champagne or sparkling white wine
2 lemons, sliced thinly

Punches, cups & toddies

Method:

Put the block of ice in the punch bowl and pour the sherry, brandy, lager and stout over the block.

Stir the mixture thoroughly and add the lemon slices.

At the last minute before serving, pour in the champagne or sparkling wine.

Serve in a ballon or wine glass (officers and gentlemen). Other ranks might enjoy it in a beer mug!

English bishop (hot)

*This is a port-wine drink, made with baked oranges
and served hot. Serves six.*

Variation:

Replace the port with red wine for a cardinal.
For a very fancy version called the *Bishop à la
Prusse*, let the roasted orange stand in the red
wine for a day. Then press out the orange juice
and reheat the whole mixture.

Ingredients:

1 large orange

12 cloves

700 ml (1¼ pints)
inexpensive port

1 tablespoon honey

1 teaspoon allspice

2 dashes cognac (optional)

Punches, cups & toddies

Method:

Stick the cloves into the whole orange
and bake it in the oven on a low heat
for 30 minutes.

Cut the baked orange into quarters
and put it into the saucepan. Pour in
the port and add the allspice, honey
and cognac if desired.

Over a very low flame, simmer gently for
15–20 minutes – do not boil or the flavour of
the port will be spoiled.

Serve in warmed cups.

Fruit-juice cup (cold)

*This is a great basic recipe with which to adapt
and experiment. Try adding exotic fruit and juices or even
adding a little more rum.*

Ingredients:

700 ml (1 bottle or 1¼ pints)
red Lambrusco (sparkling
red wine)
100 ml (4 fl oz) dark rum
500 ml (1 pint) orange juice
100 ml (4 fl oz) lemon juice
200 ml (8 fl oz) pineapple
juice
100 ml (4 fl oz) gomme syrup
1 litre (1¾ pints) ginger ale
slices of orange and lemon

Punches, cups & toddies

Method:

Chill all the ingredients first and then pour
them all into the punch bowl.
Add a block of ice and garnish with the slices
of fruit.
Serve in chilled ballon or wine glasses.

method:	PUNCH BOWL
glass:	BALLON OR WINE GLASS

Fresh-fruit punch (cold)

A festival of fruit flavours. This will serve 12 people and will give them something healthy to nibble on. It's a recipe that needs time, however, as the fruit needs to steep in the rum for at least six hours before the punch is properly prepared.

Ingredients:

block of ice

60 cl (15 fl oz) of fresh fruit – either one variety or mixed fruits

500 ml (1 pint) gomme syrup

350 ml (12 fl oz) white rum

700 ml (1¼ pint) gin

2 × 750 ml bottles of dry white wine (2⅔ pints in total)

Punches, cups & toddies

Method:

Wash and slice the fresh fruit and place it in a large bowl. Pour the gomme syrup and rum over the fruit and place it in the refrigerator for at least six hours.

Put the block of ice into the punch bowl and pour the 'marinated' fruit and liquid over the ice. Add the gin and the white wine and stir thoroughly.

Let the mix stand for a few minutes before serving in ballons or wine glasses.

Grog (hot)

This spiced-rum mix was named after Admiral Sir Edward Vernon, who was nicknamed 'Old Grog' because his cloak was made of the coarse material, grosgrain. Returning from the Caribbean in 1740, in order to save on costs (or perhaps stretch the rum ration), Old Grog diluted the crew's rum with water, a mixture that was immediately named 'Grog'. They soon discovered that it tasted better hot.

Ingredients for one cup:

2 measures dark rum

2 measures water

⅔ measure lime juice

1 teaspoon brown sugar
(or honey)

2 cloves

1 small cinnamon stick

Punches, cups & toddies

Method:

Add all of the ingredients to a small saucepan and heat gently to dissolve the sugar. When hot, strain into a heat-proof cup.

| method: | SAUCEPAN |
| glass: | HEAT-PROOF GOBLET |

Gluhwein (hot)

In German, Glühwein *means 'glowing wine' and it is a popular* après ski *drink. In Britain, it is more commonly known as mulled wine and is often served at winter parties. There are 'ready-mixed' mulled-wine spice mixes available, but it is easy (and cheaper) to make your own. You can make Glühwein in quantity as a hot punch – multiply the ingredients by the number of people.* Prosit!

Ingredients:

4 measures red wine

½ measure brandy

1 teaspoon castor sugar

1 slice orange

1 slice lemon

1 cinnamon stick

2 cloves

Punches, cups & toddies

Method:

Place all the ingredients into a saucepan and simmer gently – do not boil – for 30 minutes.

Strain into the heat-proof goblet

Hot buttered rum (hot)

*This lime-flavour cocktail was invented in the 1920s.
Originally it was served 'straight up' without the sugar. It is also
sometimes served in an old-fashioned glass filled with broken ice.
Try the variations for yourself.*

Ingredients:

2 measures dark rum

2½ measures water

1 teaspoon brown sugar
(or honey)

1 pinch ground nutmeg

4 drops vanilla essence

1 small cinnamon stick

1 small knob of butter

Punches, cups & toddies

Method:

Place the cinnamon stick,
nutmeg and vanilla essence
in the heat-proof cup.
Heat the rum, water and
sugar in the saucepan
until almost boiling.
Remove from the heat and
pour into the cup over the
spices. Put the knob of butter
on top and watch it melt into
the mixture.

method:	BUILD
glass:	HEAT-PROOF CUP
garnish:	GRATED NUTMEG

Hot Scotch toddy (hot)

Ingredients:

2 measures Scotch

3 measures boiling water

½ measure lemon juice

1 teaspoon brown sugar (or honey)

3 drops bitters

1 slice lemon, studded with cloves

ground nutmeg

Punches, cups & toddies

Method:

Put the sugar, bitters, lemon juice and clove-studded lemon slice in the glass.

Add the Scotch and pour in the boiling water. Stir to dissolve the sugar and sprinkle with ground nutmeg.

Independence Day punch (cold)

Just the thing for 4 July. Serves around 15 patriots!

Ingredients:

1 block ice
1 bottle chilled champagne or
sparkling white wine
(750 ml or 1¼ pints)
750 ml (1¼ pints) brandy
2.25 litres (3 x 750 ml bottles)
dry red wine
500 ml (1 pint) strong black
tea, chilled
juice of 24 lemons
900 g (2 lb) sugar
lemon slices

Punches, cups & toddies

Method:

In a large punch bowl, dissolve the sugar in
the lemon juice. Add the chilled tea and a
block of ice.
Pour in the red wine and the brandy.
Chill thoroughly.
Immediately before serving, add the
champagne or sparkling white wine.
Serve in ballons or wine goblets and garnish
with the lemon slices.

method:	PUNCH BOWL
glass:	FLUTE OR WINE GLASS

Lafayette punch (cold)

This is an extremely simple champagne punch, and there's enough here to serve 20 people.

Ingredients:

1 block ice
6 oranges, sliced
sugar (enough to cover the
orange slices)
1 bottle dry white wine
(750 ml or 1¼ pints)
4 bottles champagne or
sparkling white wine
(3 litres or 5¼ pints)

Punches, cups & toddies

Method:

Slice the oranges and arrange them on the
bottom of the punch bowl.
Sprinkle the orange slices with plenty of
sugar. Pour in the white wine and let the
oranges 'stand' for an hour or so.
Just before serving, add a block of ice and
pour in the chilled champagne or sparkling
white wine.

Manhattan punch (cold)

This Manhattan-style punch will serve around 12 people.

Ingredients:

1 block ice
(or some large chunks)
750 ml (1¼ pints) rosso
vermouth
1.5 litres (2⅔ pints) whisky
600 ml (21 fl oz) iced water
½ teaspoon bitters
2 oranges, sliced thinly
12 maraschino cherries
(optional)

Punches, cups & toddies

Method:

Put the block of ice into the punch bowl.
Pour the vermouth, bitters and whisky over
the ice. Add the iced water and stir
thoroughly.
Garnish with the orange slices and serve
each glass with a cherry.

method:	BUILD
glass:	HEAT-PROOF IRISH-COFFEE GLASS

Royale coffee (hot)

The most famous hot coffee and liqueur drink topped with whipped cream is Irish coffee. This uses Irish whiskey, but there are numerous variations. Try the royale, with cognac.

Variations:

Replace the cognac in the following:

tropical coffee: 1 measure golden rum and sprinkle with cinnamon;

Caribbean coffee: 1 measure dark rum and sprinkle with chocolate;

Gaelic coffee: ¾ measure Scotch and sprinkle with chocolate.

Ingredients:

1 measure cognac

5 measures hot black coffee (sweetened to taste)

1½ measures whipped cream

grated chocolate

Punches, cups & toddies

Method:

To the warmed glass, add the hot coffee and the cognac.

Gently float the whipped cream on top and sprinkle with grated chocolate.

Sangria (cold)

Once again, there are numerous versions of this famous Spanish punch. This basic recipe will keep 12 people happy, and you can add a measure or two of a liqueur if you want to experiment!
Viva Espana!

Ingredients:

ice cubes
750 ml (1¼ pints) red wine
(preferably Spanish)
4 measures brandy
(Spanish if possible)
200 ml (7 fl oz) soda water
or lemonade
juice 1 lemon
juice 1 orange
1 orange, 1 lemon, sliced
1 lime, sliced
1 tablespoon castor sugar
(or to taste)

Punches, cups & toddies

Method:

Half-fill a jug or pitcher with ice.
Add the orange and lemon juices and
dissolve the sugar.
Pour in the wine and the brandy. Add
the sliced citrus fruit, then the soda
or lemonade.
Stir and serve immediately.

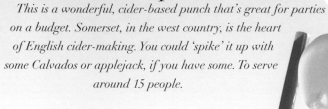

method:	PUNCH BOWL
glass:	BALLON OR WINE GLASS
garnish:	SLICED STRAWBERRIES OR APPLE SLICES

Ingredients:

1 block ice

1 litre (1¾ pints) dry cider

150 ml (5 fl oz) dry white wine

2 measures brandy (Calvados or applejack if desired)

300 ml (10 fl oz) ginger ale

150 ml (5 fl oz) orange juice

150 ml (5 fl oz) apple juice

2 measures lemon juice

sliced strawberries or apple slices

Somerset punch (cold)

This is a wonderful, cider-based punch that's great for parties on a budget. Somerset, in the west country, is the heart of English cider-making. You could 'spike' it up with some Calvados or applejack, if you have some. To serve around 15 people.

Punches, cups & toddies

Method:

Put the block of ice into the punch bowl and pour in the lemon juice, apple and orange juice.

Add the cider and the brandy (optional) and the ginger ale.

Garnish with some strawberry slices or apple slices.

Toledo punch (cold)

This is a punch devised by Harry Johnson in 1882. It's for a really big celebration and will serve 90 of your closest friends! Try this when you win the lottery!

Ingredients:

225 g (½ lb) sugar
(or more to taste)
1 litre (1¾ pints) soda water
juice of 2 lemons
500 ml (1 pint) cognac
1 small bunch mint sprigs
2 oranges, sliced thinly into
half rings
½ pineapple – diced
6 strawberries, halved

Punches, cups & toddies

Method:

Put all of the above in a large (very large!)
punchbowl and dissolve the sugar. Now add:
3 litres (5.3 pints) water
500 ml (1 pint) ordinary brandy
2 x 750 ml (25fl oz) bottles claret
2 x 750 ml (25fl oz) bottles white wine
(Johnson's recipe called for German Rhine
wine)
3 x 750 ml (25fl oz) bottles champagne
Add a block of ice and serve in ballon or wine
glasses.

Mocktails

Many people don't drink alcohol. It may be for medical or dietary reasons or because of religious beliefs. It may be because they are driving, or that they just don't like the taste of alcohol. Some people may be allergic to alcohol, some might be 'in recovery' and some might just not want a drink at that moment. Some might be under age. Whatever the reasons, if someone says 'no thanks' to a cocktail, then don't press one on them. There are lots of wonderful-tasting and good-looking 'mocktails' to be offered instead.

With many mixed drinks, mocktails included, it's almost impossible to tell whether there is alcohol in them or not just by looking at them. If you're providing drinks for a number of people, make sure you know your ingredients. Read the labels on the bottles: many so-called 'non-alcoholic' beers do, in fact, contain a small amount of alcohol. Adding a dash of bitters to a glass of tonic water also means you've added alcohol, even if it is only a very tiny amount.

There are hundreds of delicious mocktails to be enjoyed: some were specially designed, others, like the Virgin Mary (a bloody Mary without the Vodka) a Virgin Colada (a Pina Colada without the rum) or a Virgin Bellini (a Bellini without the champagne) are non-alcoholic versions of famous cocktails and very easy to make.

If you serve mocktails, then they should look just as appealing as their alcoholic cousins. Take the same care over ingre-

Tail feathers
see page 249.

dients and the same time and effort over their presentation. After all, the non-drinkers have been invited and you want them to have as good a time as the rest of your friends!

Many of the recipes in this section are ideal for children to make. Kids are entranced by the bright colours, zany names, the mixing and, above all, the umbrellas associated with cocktails, so why not let them create a few of their own? Fruity drinks are certainly more healthy than sugar-filled, fizzy concoctions, but using 'diet' versions of cola and lemonade will reduce the sugar intake if that is something that concerns you.

It might be sensible to invest in some clear plastic beakers rather than using your finest cocktail glasses, and make sure you have plenty of straws and umbrellas!

Bora-Bora
see page 234.

method:	BUILD
glass:	HIGHBALL
garnish:	SLICE OF ORANGE AND A CHERRY

Atomic cat

It looks a little like a mimosa (page 198) and tastes just as good.

Ingredients:

ice cubes

4 measures orange juice

4 measures tonic water

1 slice orange

1 maraschino cherry

Mocktails

Method:

Almost fill a highball glass
with ice cubes and pour in
the orange juice.

Add the tonic water and
garnish with the slice of
orange and the cherry.

Add a stirrer and serve.

Batman cocktail

Because Robin's legs weren't long enough to reach the pedals of the Batmobile, the Caped Crusader had to do the driving.

Ingredients:

ice cubes

6 measures orange juice

½ teaspoon grenadine

1 orange slice

Mocktails

Method:

Nearly fill the Collins glass with ice cubes.
Pour in the orange juice. Add the grenadine and stir well.
Garnish with the orange slice.
Serve with a stirrer.

Bora-Bora

Bora-Bora is in the Society Islands, part of French Polynesia in the Pacific Ocean, north west of Tahiti. Try this pineapple-flavour mocktail and conjure up images of swaying palm trees and tropical beaches.

Ingredients:

ice cubes

3 measures pineapple juice

3 measures dry ginger ale

½ measure grenadine

1 teaspoon lime juice

1 slice lime

1 maraschino cherry

Mocktails

Method:

Half-fill the shaker with ice cubes and pour in the pineapple juice, lime juice and grenadine.

Shake well and strain into an ice-filled glass.

Top with the dry ginger ale and garnish with the slice of lime and the cherry.

Serve with straws.

Brontosaurus

*A long drink, as befitting the dinosaur with
the very long neck! The Greek word dinosaur means
'terrible lizard', and the
celery-stick garnish is a tribute
to the herbivorous diet
of this long-extinct
giant.*

Ingredients:

ice cubes

3 measures grapefruit juice

½ measure lime juice

½ measure grenadine

3 measures lemonade

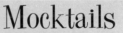

Mocktails

Method:

Half-fill the shaker with ice
cubes and pour in the lime
juice, grapefruit juice and
grenadine.

Shake well and strain into an
ice-filled highball glass and
top with the lemonade.

Garnish with the celery stick
(optional).

method:	SHAKER
glass:	HIGHBALL
garnish:	SLICE OF LEMON

Cinderella

This delicious, long, fruity drink is the real reason why Cinders stayed too long at the ball! You can drink it from a glass slipper if you want.

Ingredients:

ice cubes

2 measures orange juice

2 measures pineapple juice

1 measure lemon juice

½ measure gomme syrup

1 measure soda water

Mocktails

Method:

Half-fill the shaker with ice cubes and add the orange and pineapple juice, the lemon juice and the gomme syrup.

Shake well and strain into an ice-filled highball glass and top with soda.

Garnish with the slice of lemon and serve with straws.

Cranberry cooler

A great colour and a lovely, dry taste.

Ingredients:

ice cubes

4 measures cranberry juice

2 measures red grape juice

2 measures lemon-lime soda

1 lime wedge

Mocktails

Method:

Put some ice cubes in a highball glass and pour on the cranberry juice and red grape juice.

Top with the lemon-lime soda and stir well.

Garnish with the lime wedge and serve with a stirrer.

method:	SHAKER
glass:	HIGHBALL
garnish:	LIME WEDGE

Flamingo

*Long, elegant and pink
– just like the bird.*

Ingredients:

ice cubes

4 measures cranberry juice

2 measures pineapple juice

½ measure lemon juice

2 measures soda water

1 lime wedge

Mocktails

Method:

Half-fill the shaker with ice cubes.

Pour in the cranberry and pineapple juices and add the lemon juice.

Shake well and strain into ice-filled highball glass.

Top with the soda water and garnish with the lime wedge.

Lassi

*Nothing to do with that incredibly clever dog, a lassi is
an Indian drink made with yoghurt. As well as being refreshing,
it's also very versatile. You can make it plain,
salted or sweet, or add fruit.*

Ingredients:

ice cubes
2 measures plain yoghurt
6 measures cold water
pinch of salt
sprinkle of roasted cumin
seeds

Variations:

Sweet lassi
Omit the salt and add 2
teaspoons granulated sugar
and 2 drops rosewater.
Whizz in the blender and
pour into an ice-filled
Collins glass.

Fruity lassi
Replace the water with 5
measures fruit juice and 1
measure lemon juice.
Try pineapple, cranberry,
mango or passionfruit
juice.

Mocktails

Method:

Place the yoghurt, water and
salt in the blender and blend
thoroughly.
Pour into an ice-filled highball
glass and add the cumin
seeds.
Stir well and serve with a
stirrer.

method:	BUILD
glass:	HIGHBALL
garnish:	2 CHERRIES AND GRATED CHOCOLATE

Mickey Mouse

More an ice-cream float than a mocktail, but if you a) can remember all of the words to the Mickey Mouse Club song; b) ever had a Mouseketeer's hat with your name on it; or c) are a man who still has dreams in which Annette Funicello plays a major part, then you have every right to enjoy this!

Ingredients:

5 measures cold cola
1 scoop vanilla (or your
favourite flavour) ice cream
1 measure whipped cream
2 maraschino cherries
grated chocolate

Mocktails

Method:

Put the cold cola into the
highball glass and float the ice
cream on top.
Add the whipped cream and
garnish with the two
cherries. Liberally dust with
grated chocolate.
Add straws and a spoon.
Lock the door, take the
phone off the hook and vow
that you will go to the gym
one day soon!

Pink lemonade

This is so easy to make – you can make a jugful
and play around with the ingredients as well.

Ingredients:

ice cubes
1½ measures lemon juice
1½ measures gomme syrup
⅓ measure grenadine
4 measures ice-cold water

Variations:

For fizzy pink lemonade,
replace the cold water with
cold soda water. Add the soda
to the glass after the other
ingredients have been shaken
and strained.

For limeade, simply replace the
lemon juice with lime juice.

For orangeade, replace the
lemon juice with orange juice.

Mocktails

Method:

Half-fill the shaker with ice
cubes.
Pour in the lemon juice,
water, grenadine and gomme
syrup and shake well.
Strain into an ice-filled
highball glass and garnish with
the lemon slice and cherry.

method:	BUILD
glass:	HIGHBALL
garnish:	SLICE OF LIME AND A CHERRY

Pomola

Very simple to make and a welcome change from a 'straight' iced cola.

Ingredients:

ice cubes

5 measures cold cola

1 measure lime juice

⅓ measure grenadine

1 slice lime

1 maraschino cherry

Mocktails

Method:

Put some ice cubes in a highball glass.

Pour in the cold cola, the lime juice and the grenadine. Stir gently and garnish with the slice of lime and cherry. Serve with straws and a stirrer.

Prohibition punch

This is a great party drink, especially if there are a lot of people and it's a mixed crowd. This recipe will serve around six people.

Ingredients:

ice cubes

3 measures lemon juice

1 measure gomme syrup

225 ml (½ pint) apple juice

500ml (1 pint) ginger ale

orange slices

Mocktails

Method:

Put some ice cubes in the jug or pitcher.

Pour in the lemon juice, apple juice and gomme syrup and stir gently.

Pour in the ginger ale.

Serve in ice-filled highball glasses and garnish with an orange slice.

method:	BUILD
glass:	HIGHBALL
garnish:	SPIRAL OF LEMON PEEL

Rail splitter

A good Prohibition cooler.

Ingredients:

ice cubes

1 measure lemon juice

¾ measure gomme syrup

4 measures ginger ale

Mocktails

Method:

Put some ice cubes in a highball glass.

Pour in the lemon juice, gomme syrup and top with the ginger ale and stir gently.

Garnish with a spiral of lemon peel.

Roy Rogers

Named after Hollywood's most famous singing cowboy, whose real name was, in fact, Leonard Slye.

Ingredients:

ice cubes

4 measures ginger ale

2 measures lemon-lime soda

1 teaspoon grenadine

1 orange slice

1 maraschino cherry

Mocktails

Method:

Put some ice cubes into a highball glass and pour in the ginger ale, lemon-lime soda and grenadine.

Stir well and garnish with the cherry and orange slice.

246

method:	BUILD
glass:	CHAMPAGNE SAUCER OR HIGHBALL
garnish:	MARASCHINO CHERRY, SLICE OF ORANGE

Shirley Temple

A number of celebrities have given their names to mixed drinks and cocktails: novelist Ernest Hemingway, actresses Rosalind Russell and Marjorie King (the Margarita), artist Charles Gibson and the millionaire Colonel Cornelius Vanderbilt are just a few. Some people think that all mocktails are called 'Shirley Temples' after the child star (and later American diplomat). For purists (and film buffs) however, there is, and only ever will be, one Shirley Temple.

Mocktails

method:

Champagne saucer: Fill the chilled saucer with the cold lemon-lime soda or ginger ale. Add the grenadine and garnish with the cherry and orange slice.

Highball: Place some ice cubes in the highball glass. Pour in the lemon-lime soda or ginger ale. Add the grenadine and stir well. Garnish with the cherry and orange slice

Ingredients:

ice cubes (if served in a highball)
5 measures cold lemon-lime soda
or 5 measures cold ginger ale
1 teaspoon grenadine
1 maraschino cherry
1 slice orange

Southern ginger

A non-alcoholic version of the mint julep.

Ingredients:

broken ice

5 measures dry ginger ale

½ measure gomme syrup

½ measure lemon juice

2 sprigs of mint (1 for garnish)

Mocktails

Method:

Put one sprig of mint into the highball glass and gently crush it to squeeze out some juice. Two-thirds fill the glass with broken ice and pour in the lemon juice, gomme syrup and ginger ale.

Mix gently.

Garnish with the remaining sprig of mint and serve with straws and a muddler.

method:	BUILD
glass:	HIGHBALL
garnish:	SLICES OF ORANGE AND LEMON

St Clements

'Oranges and lemons, say the bells of St Clement's'.

Ingredients:

broken ice

2 measures orange juice

2 measures sparkling
bitter lemon

1 slice orange

1 slice lemon

Mocktails

Method:

Two-thirds fill the highball
glass with broken ice.
Pour in the orange juice and
add the sparkling bitter
lemon.
Garnish with the orange and
lemon slices and serve with
straws.

Tail Feathers

This Prohibition highball uses ginger beer.

Ingredients:

ice cubes

1 measure orange juice

5 measures ginger beer
(not ginger ale)

1 sprig mint

1 lime slice

Mocktails

Method:

Put some ice cubes in the
highball glass.
Pour in the orange juice and
add the ginger beer.
Garnish with the sprig of
mint and the lime slice.

method:	BLENDER
glass:	HIGHBALL
garnish:	SLICE OF ORANGE AND A CHERRY

Tarzan's juicy cooler

Another great mocktail that makes excellent use of yoghurt.

Ingredients:

3 measures orange juice

3 measures pineapple juice

¼ measure grenadine

½ measure lemon juice

2 measures yoghurt (plain or fruit flavoured)

1 teaspoon (or more to taste) clear honey

1 orange slice

1 maraschino cherry

Mocktails

Method:

Put half a glassful of crushed ice into the blender.

Pour in the orange juice, pineapple juice, grenadine, lemon juice, yoghurt and honey.

Blend briefly and pour into a highball glass.

Garnish with the orange slice and the maraschino cherry.

Serve with straws.

Virgin Bellini

You can make this with peach nectar or by 'crushing' a peeled and de-stoned peach in a blender.

Ingredients:

3 measures peach nectar
(or crush 1 large, ripe
peach – peeled and
de-stoned – in a blender)
1 teaspoon grenadine
1 measure lemon juice
4 measures chilled soda water

Mocktails

Method:

Into a chilled champagne
flute, pour the peach nectar.
Add the grenadine and lemon
juice and top with the chilled
soda water.
Stir well.

Yellowjacket

A yellowjacket is a type of wasp, so be prepared for quite
a sharp 'sting' of a drink!

Ingredients:

ice cubes

2 measures pineapple juice

2 measures orange juice

1½ measures lemon juice

Mocktails

Method:

Half-fill the shaker with ice
cubes.
Pour in the lemon juice,
orange juice and pineapple
juice and shake well.
Strain into an ice-filled old-
fashioned glass.

Index

Bibliography

Salvatore Calabrese, *Classic Cocktails*, Prion, 1997

Gary Regan, *The Bartender's Bible*, HarperCollins, 1993

Harry's ABC of Mixing Cocktails, Harry MacElhone with Andrew MacElhone,
Souvenir Press, 1986

Gino Marcialis & Franco Zingalis, *The Cocktail Book*, MacDonald, 1983

Michael Jackson, *Michael Jackson's Pocket Bar Book*, Mitchell Beazley, 1981

David A. Embury, *The Fine Art of Mixing Drinks*, Faber, 1963

Ambrose Heath, *Good Drinks*, Faber, 1939

Credits and Acknowledgements

Additional photography by
STEPHEN BRAYNE.

Special thanks to
NICK LAWES.

All glassware and cocktail equipment supplied by:
GILL WING,
Upper Street, Islington, London.